THE CRYPTO COMPASS: CHARTING YOUR PATH IN A DIGITAL WORLD

From Basics to Breakthroughs: Building Wealth in the Digital Age

Theo Quantum

IDEAL PRODUCT SOLUTIONS

CONTENTS

Title Page
Chapter 1. Understanding the Basics of Cryptocurrency — 12
Chapter 2: Exploring Different Types of Cryptocurrencies — 22
Chapter 3: Setting Up Your First Crypto Wallet — 37
Chapter 4: Getting Started on Crypto Exchanges — 51
Chapter 5: Making Your First Crypto Purchase — 61
Chapter 6: Managing Risks in Crypto Investing — 76
Chapter 7: Understanding Crypto Taxes and Regulations — 96
Chapter 8: Building a Long-Term Crypto Strategy — 112
Chapter 9: Staying Updated in the Crypto World — 126
Chapter 10: The Future of Cryptocurrency and Your Role as an Investor — 141

Disclaimer

This book is intended solely for educational and informational purposes and does not constitute financial or investment advice. The information provided here aims to offer a foundational understanding of cryptocurrency, digital currency, and blockchain technology, along with general insights into digital asset markets. It is not meant to recommend or endorse any specific investment strategy, currency, or asset.

Investing in cryptocurrency involves significant risk, and past performance does not guarantee future results. Readers should perform due diligence and consult a qualified financial or investment advisor before making investment decisions. The author, publisher, and any affiliates are not responsible for any monetary losses or gains that may result from using the information provided in this book.

By continuing to read, you acknowledge that this book is an educational resource only, and any investment choices you make are at your own risk.

Preface

The world of finance is undergoing a revolution, and you are standing at the cusp of a transformative moment. Imagine a system where you control your money, financial transactions are borderless, secure, and transparent, and where technology empowers millions to achieve financial independence. This is not a distant dream but the reality of cryptocurrency—a groundbreaking shift in how we think about, interact with, and manage money. Welcome to your crypto adventure.

You've likely heard the buzz about cryptocurrency—maybe through headlines proclaiming Bitcoin's meteoric rise, friends debating Ethereum's latest innovations, or even cautionary tales of volatility. It might seem like a mysterious or intimidating space reserved for tech-savvy early adopters or daring investors. The truth, however, is that cryptocurrency is for everyone. It is a movement transcending borders, demographics, and industries, shaping the future of finance in ways we are only beginning to understand.

This book, The Crypto Compass: Charting Your Path in a Digital World, is your guide to navigating this exciting and complex landscape. Whether you're an absolute beginner curious about the fuss, a seasoned investor looking to deepen your knowledge, or someone simply eager to stay ahead of the curve, this journey is for you. Together, we'll demystify cryptocurrency, explore its potential, and equip you with the tools and confidence to make informed decisions.

Cryptocurrency is more than just digital money; it's a technological breakthrough that has implications far beyond finance. At its core is blockchain technology—a decentralized, immutable ledger that enables secure and transparent transactions. This innovation has opened new opportunities, from decentralized finance (DeFi) and non-fungible tokens (NFTs) to supply chain optimization and global data security.

But what does this mean for you, the individual? It means financial independence, democratization of wealth, and the chance to participate in a global economy that is increasingly digital and decentralized. Cryptocurrency empowers you to take control of your financial future, offering alternatives to traditional banking systems that can be restrictive, costly, and inequitable.

Picture this: sending money to a friend halfway across the world in minutes without worrying about high fees or currency exchange rates. Or imagine investing in innovative projects during their early stages, once an opportunity reserved only for the wealthy elite. Cryptocurrency makes this possible, and it's just the beginning.

Access to traditional financial systems is limited or nonexistent for billions of people worldwide. Banks, credit institutions, and investment platforms often require geographic proximity, credit histories, or substantial wealth to participate. Cryptocurrency breaks down these barriers. You only need an internet connection and a digital wallet to access financial tools and opportunities.

This inclusivity is perhaps one of cryptocurrency's most profound impacts. It provides unbanked and underbanked populations a way to save, transact, and invest. It levels the playing field, enabling people from diverse backgrounds to build wealth, create businesses, and achieve financial security. As cryptocurrency continues to evolve, its potential to drive global financial inclusion cannot be overstated. At the heart of cryptocurrency lies blockchain technology—a system that records transactions across multiple computers in a secure, transparent, and tamper-proof way. While its initial application was to power Bitcoin, blockchain's potential extends far beyond digital currency. It's revolutionizing healthcare, logistics, real estate, and even voting systems.

Blockchain's strength lies in its ability to create trust in a trustless environment. Imagine a world where supply chains are fully transparent, ensuring ethical sourcing of goods; where medical records are secure yet accessible to authorized parties; or elections are tamper-proof, restoring faith in democratic processes. These are not abstract possibilities, but real-world applications are being implemented today. By understanding cryptocurrency, you're also gaining insight into the broader implications of blockchain technology. This knowledge positions you at the forefront of innovation, enabling you to participate in shaping the future of industries and institutions.

Of course, no adventure comes without its challenges. Cryptocurrency is a volatile and fast-moving market, with opportunities for significant gains and risks of substantial losses. Stories of overnight millionaires are matched by cautionary tales of those who lost it all in speculative frenzies. Understanding the fundamentals and approaching the market with a strategic mindset is essential. This book will help you navigate the risks while seizing the opportunities. We'll cover everything from setting up a digital wallet to advanced strategies for evaluating blockchain projects. You'll learn to spot trends, avoid scams, and make decisions rooted in knowledge rather than hype. While there are no guarantees in investing, preparation and education are your best tools for success.

The cryptocurrency world is vast and multifaceted, encompassing diverse projects, communities, and technologies. Bitcoin and Ethereum may dominate the headlines, but they are just the tip of the iceberg. Decentralized finance platforms, NFTs, stablecoins, and emerging blockchain networks each offer unique opportunities and challenges.

Engaging with this ecosystem also means connecting with its communities. The crypto space thrives on collaboration and shared knowledge. From Reddit forums and Twitter discussions to Discord channels and Telegram groups, these communities are hubs of innovation and insight. Participating in these networks gives you access to real-time information, expert opinions, and the collective wisdom of passionate enthusiasts.

The Crypto Compass is designed to be more than just a guide; it's a tool for empowerment. Each chapter will equip you with practical advice, real-world examples, and actionable steps to chart your course in the digital world. Whether you're looking to invest, build, or understand, this book will help you confidently navigate the complexities of cryptocurrency. We'll begin by demystifying the basics—what cryptocurrency is, how it works, and why it matters. We'll delve into investment strategies, technological trends, and emerging opportunities from there. Along the way, you'll gain the tools to assess risks, evaluate projects, and make informed decisions tailored to your goals.

The future of cryptocurrency is still being written, and your role in shaping it is significant. As blockchain technology continues to disrupt traditional systems, those who are informed and adaptable will be best positioned to thrive. By embarking on this journey, you're not just learning about cryptocurrency; you're engaging with a transformative movement that has the potential to redefine our financial, technological, and social landscapes.

The road ahead may be uncertain, but it is filled with possibility. As you navigate this adventure, remember that the most important investment you can make is in yourself—your knowledge, skills, and ability to adapt. This book is here to guide you every step of the way, providing the tools and insights you need to succeed.

Welcome to the world of cryptocurrency. The compass is in your hands. Let's chart your path together.

Introduction

The world of cryptocurrency is buzzing with energy, innovation, and opportunity. Digital currency is changing how we think about money, ownership, and freedom. And you're here, about to start your journey, taking your first step into one of our time's most exciting and transformative revolutions. Whether you're curious about crypto, you want to understand blockchain technology, or you're considering investing in digital assets, this book is your companion, breaking down the essentials in a way that's easy, engaging, and actionable.

Why Cryptocurrency? Why Now?

You might wonder, "Why is everyone suddenly so obsessed with cryptocurrency?" Well, crypto isn't just about money; it's about reimagining what money could be. Traditional currencies are controlled by governments and regulated by banks, which means borders, politics, and the ebb and flow of economic policies bind them. Cryptocurrency, on the other hand, is different. It's decentralized, meaning no central authority controls it. It's global, accessible to anyone with an internet connection, and powered by blockchain technology, providing transparency, security, and, for many, a sense of financial freedom.

Imagine instantly sending money globally without worrying about exchange rates, banking hours, or transfer fees. Imagine investing directly in groundbreaking new technologies and startups because you hold a few digital tokens. These aren't just pipe dreams; they're real possibilities in cryptocurrency. While there are risks (we'll talk a lot about them), crypto's opportunities and freedom make it revolutionary.

What You'll Find in This Book
This book isn't here to sell you on a get-rich-quick fantasy, nor will it overload you with complex jargon or technical details. Instead, think of it as a roadmap. We'll start from scratch and work our way up, step-by-step, so you can feel confident, empowered, and well-prepared to explore the crypto universe.

I'm here to help you understand how crypto works, why it's caught the world's attention, and how you might begin your journey into this digital landscape. By the end, you'll have the knowledge and tools to make decisions, build a thoughtful approach to crypto investing, and, most importantly, avoid the pitfalls many newcomers face.

Each chapter builds on the last, covering everything from understanding the core technology behind cryptocurrencies to setting up a secure wallet, making your first crypto purchase, and developing a long-term strategy. Whether you're interested in investing in Bitcoin, exploring up-and-coming altcoins, or staying informed, this book will give you the foundational knowledge you need.

Setting Expectations and Staying Smart

If you're like most newcomers, you may have heard stories about people who made fortunes with crypto and others who lost big. Both can be true. Crypto markets are notoriously volatile, meaning prices can swing wildly in short amounts of time. This volatility is one of the factors that makes crypto both exciting and risky. But here's the secret: understanding the market, managing risk, and setting realistic expectations will set you apart from those chasing the next big "moonshot."

In this book, you won't find specific financial advice or promises of "secret strategies" to become an overnight millionaire. Instead, you'll find insights on navigating the space responsibly and safely, with your eyes open to the risks and rewards. The journey might be thrilling, but it's important to remember that success in crypto, as in any investment, takes patience, knowledge, and careful planning.

How This Book is Structured

To make this journey as smooth and enjoyable as possible, the book is divided into ten chapters, each focused on a critical aspect of cryptocurrency investing:

Chapter 1. Understanding the Basics of Cryptocurrency – We start with the essentials: what cryptocurrency is, why it exists, and how it's changing the game in finance.

Chapter 2. Exploring Different Types of Cryptocurrencies – Here, we'll look at Bitcoin, Ethereum, and other popular coins, including stablecoins and altcoins, so that you can understand the diversity within the crypto world.

Chapter 3. Setting Up Your First Crypto Wallet – Consider this your digital bank account. We'll guide you through the different types of wallets and help you choose the one that's right for you.

Chapter 4. Getting Started on Crypto Exchanges – Exchanges are like marketplaces for crypto. We'll cover how to pick a reliable one, set up your account, and secure your transactions.

Chapter 5. Making Your First Crypto Purchase – Ready to dive in? This chapter will take you through your first transaction step-by-step.

Chapter 6. Managing Risks in Crypto Investing – Crypto is thrilling but has risks. Here, we'll discuss ways to protect yourself and manage those risks safely.

Chapter 7. Understanding Crypto Taxes and Regulations – Every investor needs to stay compliant. This chapter will walk you through the basics of crypto taxes and regulations.

Chapter 8. Building a Long-Term Crypto Strategy – Think beyond the short term. Here, we'll discuss strategies for growing and managing a crypto portfolio.

Chapter 9. Staying Updated in the Crypto World – Crypto evolves fast. We'll cover ways to keep up with news, trends, and developments.

Chapter 10. The Future of Cryptocurrency and Your Role as an Investor – Finally, we will explore emerging trends and technologies and how you can continue to grow with the industry.

A Beginner's Adventure
Getting into crypto is like learning to ride a bike. At first, you may feel wobbly, unsure, and maybe even a bit scared. But as you practice and learn, it gets easier, and soon enough, you're riding smoothly, even enjoying the journey! Remember, starting small, taking your time, and building your confidence one step at a time is okay.

Crypto is a constantly changing landscape, and this book is designed to equip you with the knowledge and flexibility to adapt and succeed. Think of this journey as an adventure, one where you'll learn, grow, and discover new possibilities that were unimaginable just a few years ago.

Final Thoughts: Let's Get Started!
Cryptocurrency is reshaping the world of finance and creating opportunities for those willing to dive in and learn. It's not

a get-rich-quick scheme or a magic solution, but it can be a fascinating, rewarding journey with the right approach. You're about to enter a world combining cutting-edge technology, financial empowerment, and a global community of innovators.

So, are you ready to chart your path? Let's dive in and get started on this thrilling adventure. Welcome to the world of cryptocurrency investing—let the journey begin!

CHAPTER 1. UNDERSTANDING THE BASICS OF CRYPTOCURRENCY

Cryptocurrency represents a groundbreaking shift in how we think about money, finance, and technology. Its rise has revolutionized the concept of value exchange, introducing a system where digital currencies operate independently of traditional banking and government oversight. To grasp the full potential of cryptocurrency, we need to start with its fundamentals: what it is, where it came from, and the key ideas that underpin it. This chapter builds the foundation for your journey into the crypto world, providing the tools you'll need to navigate its complexities and opportunities.

What is Cryptocurrency?
At its core, cryptocurrency is a digital form of money that exists solely electronically. Unlike traditional currencies like the U.S. dollar or the euro, cryptocurrency is not tied to a central authority or government. Instead, it operates on decentralized networks powered by blockchain technology—a topic we'll explore shortly. The key to cryptocurrency's appeal lies in its ability to offer financial autonomy, privacy, and a global reach, free from the restrictions of traditional financial systems.

To illustrate the power of cryptocurrency, consider Maria, who lives in a country with limited banking services. Before cryptocurrency, sending money to her sister overseas was a slow, expensive process involving multiple intermediaries. With Bitcoin, Maria can transfer funds directly from her digital wallet to her sister's wallet in minutes, bypassing the traditional banking system entirely. This efficiency and accessibility have made cryptocurrency an invaluable tool for millions worldwide.

Cryptocurrencies are not only decentralized but also secure. Each transaction is recorded on a blockchain, an immutable digital ledger maintained by a network of computers. These transactions are verified through cryptographic processes, ensuring accuracy and preventing fraud. Unlike fiat currency, which is tied to physical assets or government decrees, the value of cryptocurrency is determined by factors like supply, demand, and the trust placed in the network.

The decentralized nature of cryptocurrency gives individuals unprecedented control over their money. If you own cryptocurrency, you hold a private key that grants you access to your funds. This key is yours alone, meaning you don't need to rely on banks or other institutions to manage your assets. For those who prioritize financial independence and privacy, this control is revolutionary.

The History and Evolution of Cryptocurrency
The idea of digital currency dates back decades, long before Bitcoin debuted. Early cryptography and computer science pioneers envisioned a form of money that could enable secure and private transactions in an increasingly digital world. However, these early efforts were limited by the inability to create a decentralized system to prevent double-spending—where the same digital asset is used more than once.

This all changed in 2008 when an anonymous figure or group known as Satoshi Nakamoto published the Bitcoin white paper titled Bitcoin: A Peer-to-Peer Electronic Cash System. Satoshi's vision was simple yet groundbreaking: a decentralized digital currency that allowed people to transact directly with one another without intermediaries like banks. In January 2009, the Bitcoin network went live, and the first Bitcoin block, known as the "genesis block," was mined.

Bitcoin's innovation lies in its use of blockchain technology—a distributed ledger that records every transaction on the network. This ledger was maintained by a decentralized network of computers, or nodes, that collectively verified and added transactions. The process of verification, called "proof of work," ensured that the network remained secure and tamper-proof. Every transaction was encrypted and immutable, building trust in a system without a central authority.

In its early days, Bitcoin was primarily used by tech enthusiasts and libertarians who valued its decentralized nature. Over time, its popularity grew, and it began to be recognized as a store of value—often referred to as "digital gold." Other developers saw Bitcoin's success and began creating their cryptocurrencies, known as altcoins. Some, like Litecoin, aimed to improve transaction speed and efficiency. In contrast, others, like Ripple, focused on specific use cases like cross-border payments.

The most significant evolution came in 2015 with the launch of Ethereum. This blockchain platform expanded the capabilities of cryptocurrency. Unlike Bitcoin, which was designed primarily as a digital currency, Ethereum introduced the concept of "smart contracts." These programmable agreements could automatically execute tasks when predefined conditions were met, opening the door to a new era of decentralized applications (dApps).

Today, the cryptocurrency landscape is vast and diverse. There are thousands of coins and tokens, each serving different purposes. Stablecoins like Tether (USDT) aim to reduce volatility by pegging their value to traditional currencies. Privacy-focused coins like Monero offer enhanced anonymity for users. Meanwhile, innovations like decentralized finance (DeFi) and non-fungible tokens (NFTs) are expanding how we use digital assets.

Key Terms and Concepts
Stepping into the cryptocurrency world can feel like learning a new language. The terms and concepts might seem overwhelming initially, but understanding them is crucial to making informed decisions as an investor. Here are some foundational ideas that will guide you through your journey.

Blockchain: At the heart of cryptocurrency lies blockchain technology. This decentralized and distributed ledger records transactions across a network of computers. Each transaction is grouped into a "block" and then added to a chain of previous blocks. This structure ensures that all transactions are secure, transparent, and irreversible. Think of it as a digital record book that everyone can see, but no one can alter.

Bitcoin (BTC): As the first and most well-known cryptocurrency, Bitcoin sets the standard for digital currency. With a capped supply of 21 million coins, Bitcoin is often compared to gold for its scarcity and role as a store of value. Its success paved the way for the development of thousands of other cryptocurrencies.

Altcoins: Any cryptocurrency other than Bitcoin is referred to as an altcoin. These range from major players like Ethereum and Cardano to smaller, experimental projects. Each altcoin serves a unique purpose, from enabling faster transactions to powering decentralized applications.

Ethereum (ETH): Ethereum is a platform that revolutionized blockchain technology by introducing smart contracts. Unlike Bitcoin, which primarily serves as a digital currency, Ethereum's blockchain allows developers to build and deploy decentralized applications. This innovation has made Ethereum a cornerstone of the DeFi movement and the broader crypto ecosystem.

Wallet: A digital wallet is where you store your cryptocurrency. Two main types are hot wallets (connected to the internet) and cold wallets (offline for maximum security). Wallets use public and private keys to facilitate transactions, with the private key acting as the secure password to access your funds.

Mining: The process of creating new cryptocurrency and verifying transactions. Miners use powerful computers to solve complex mathematical puzzles, securing the network and earning rewards in the form of cryptocurrency. Mining plays a crucial role in maintaining the integrity of proof-of-work blockchains like Bitcoin.

Stablecoins: These are cryptocurrencies designed to maintain a stable value by being pegged to traditional assets like the U.S. dollar. Stablecoins offer the benefits of cryptocurrency—speed, security, and accessibility—without the volatility.

DeFi (Decentralized Finance): DeFi refers to a financial system built on blockchain technology that operates without traditional intermediaries like banks. DeFi platforms offer decentralized alternatives to conventional financial services, from lending and borrowing to trading and insurance.

NFTs (Non-Fungible Tokens): NFTs are unique digital assets representing ownership of a specific item, such as art, music, or virtual real estate. Unlike cryptocurrencies, which are interchangeable, each NFT has its distinct value and properties.

Your Foundation for the Journey Ahead
Understanding cryptocurrency's basics is about more than learning technical details; it's about recognizing the revolutionary potential of digital money. For people like Maria, Bitcoin offers financial inclusion and freedom. For others, it represents an investment in the future of technology. By mastering the key concepts and history, you're building a foundation to guide you through this fast-moving world's complexities.

As you continue your journey, you'll encounter new technologies, trends, and opportunities. Each step will bring you closer to understanding how cryptocurrency fits into the broader landscape of finance and innovation. Next, we'll explore the many types of cryptocurrencies available today, diving deeper into their unique roles and purposes. Together, we'll build on this foundation, transforming curiosity into confidence and knowledge into action. Welcome to the world of cryptocurrency—your journey is just beginning.

Blockchain Technology Essentials

Blockchain technology is the backbone of cryptocurrency, and understanding its mechanics is essential for anyone venturing into this revolutionary space. Unlike traditional financial systems, which rely on centralized institutions like banks to maintain and verify records, blockchain operates on a decentralized network, ensuring security, transparency, and trust. This section will guide you through the essentials of blockchain technology, exploring how it works, the critical roles of miners and validators, and the innovative ways it ensures security and transparency.

How Blockchain Works

To grasp blockchain, imagine a digital ledger shared among participants worldwide. In conventional systems, a single authority, like a bank, controls ledgers. Still, blockchain flips this model on its head. Instead of one centralized entity keeping track of transactions, the ledger is distributed across a network of computers or nodes. These nodes collaborate to validate and record every transaction, ensuring that the system operates transparently and securely.

Each transaction on a blockchain is grouped with others into a "block." Think of a block as a page in a record book. It contains crucial information, such as the transaction amount, sender, and receiver. Once the block is complete, it is cryptographically linked to the previous block in the chain. This creates a chronological and immutable sequence of records that traces every transaction back to the very beginning of the network, often referred to as the "genesis block."

What makes blockchain remarkable is its decentralized nature. There's no single party in charge. Instead, every participant in the network holds a copy of the blockchain, and transactions are verified collectively. This is achieved through consensus mechanisms, which ensure that all nodes agree on the validity of transactions before they are added to the chain. The most common mechanisms are proof of work (PoW) and proof of stake (PoS). In PoW, used by Bitcoin, nodes compete to solve complex mathematical puzzles, with the winner earning the right to add the block and claim a reward. PoS, on the other hand, selects validators based on the amount of cryptocurrency they "stake" in the network, offering a more energy-efficient alternative.

This decentralized, consensus-driven model ensures accuracy and makes the blockchain highly secure and resistant to tampering. Every transaction is time-stamped and cannot be altered once recorded. This immutability is one of blockchain's most powerful features, making it ideal for applications where trust and accuracy are paramount.

The Role of Miners and Validators
Miners and validators are the unsung heroes of blockchain networks, working behind the scenes to keep these systems secure and operational. They perform the essential task of verifying transactions and adding them to the blockchain, ensuring that every entry is accurate and tamper-proof.

Miners use computational power to solve cryptographic puzzles in proof-of-work systems like Bitcoin. Picture a global race where computers compete to crack a code—the first to succeed is to add a new block to the blockchain. This process not only validates transactions but also introduces new cryptocurrencies into circulation. For example, Bitcoin miners are rewarded with BTC for their efforts. This mechanism incentivizes them to contribute computational resources to the network. However, mining requires substantial energy and hardware, which has sparked debates about its environmental impact.

In contrast, proof-of-stake systems like Ethereum's newer model rely on validators rather than miners. Validators are chosen to confirm transactions based on the amount of cryptocurrency they hold. They are willing to "stake" as collateral. If a validator acts dishonestly, they risk losing a portion of their stake, creating a strong incentive for honest behavior. Unlike mining, validating in a PoS system doesn't require massive energy consumption, making it a more sustainable alternative.

Miners and validators play a critical role in maintaining the integrity of blockchain networks. They ensure that every transaction is legitimate, preventing fraud and double-spending. By participating in this process, they contribute to the decentralized nature of the blockchain, eliminating the need for intermediaries like banks.

Security and Transparency of Blockchain
Blockchain's appeal goes beyond decentralization—it's also one of the most secure technologies available. Its combination of immutability, cryptography, and transparency creates a system where trust is built into the structure itself rather than being reliant on external authorities.

One of blockchain's standout features is immutability. Once a transaction is added to the blockchain, it cannot be altered or erased. This is achieved through cryptographic links between blocks, each containing a unique "hash" that serves as its digital fingerprint. Any attempt to change the data in a block would alter its hash, breaking the link to subsequent blocks and alerting the network to tampering. This makes blockchain ideal for use cases where a permanent, verifiable record is crucial, such as financial transactions, supply chain tracking, and identity management.

Decentralization further strengthens blockchain's security. Unlike centralized systems, which are vulnerable to single points of failure, blockchain operates on a distributed network of nodes. To compromise a blockchain, an attacker must control most of these nodes. This feat becomes increasingly difficult as the network grows. This level of attack is nearly impossible for large, well-established blockchains like Bitcoin and Ethereum due to the sheer size and computational power of their networks.

Transparency is another cornerstone of blockchain technology. Public blockchains like Bitcoin and Ethereum allow anyone to view and verify transactions. This openness ensures accountability and fosters trust among participants. For example, if Alice sends Bitcoin to Bob, anyone on the network can confirm the transaction details without seeing their personal information. Private blockchains, often used in enterprise settings, offer similar benefits but restrict access to authorized participants.

Cryptographic security underpins every aspect of blockchain. Users interact with the network through public and private keys, a pair of cryptographic codes that enable secure transactions. The public key serves as an address for receiving funds, while the private key acts as a password that grants access to the user's wallet. No one—not even the network—can access a user's funds without the private key. This cryptographic layer ensures that transactions are secure and identities are protected.

Consensus mechanisms like PoW and PoS add another layer of security. By requiring participants to expend resources —whether computational power or staked cryptocurrency—

to validate transactions, these mechanisms make fraudulent activity costly and unlikely. They also ensure the network operates smoothly and efficiently, even without a central authority.

These features make blockchain a groundbreaking solution for recording and verifying data. Its combination of security, transparency, and decentralization has applications far beyond cryptocurrency, from healthcare and real estate to voting systems and digital art.

Bringing It All Together
Blockchain technology is more than a technical innovation—it reimagines how trust and transparency can be achieved without intermediaries. By understanding how blockchain works, the roles of miners and validators, and the layers of security built into the system, you can appreciate why it serves as the foundation for cryptocurrencies and many other emerging technologies.

For someone like Sarah, a small business owner, blockchain can accept payments from international customers without relying on expensive and slow traditional banking systems. For others, like developers building decentralized applications, it provides a platform for innovation that removes barriers and empowers creativity.

As you continue exploring the crypto world, remember that blockchain's design makes it so revolutionary. It's not just about digital currency—it's about creating systems that are fair, secure, and accessible to all. Next, we'll dive into the specific types of cryptocurrencies built on blockchain technology, from Bitcoin to the altcoins that are expanding their possibilities. This journey will deepen your understanding of how blockchain powers an entire ecosystem of digital assets and opportunities.

CHAPTER 2: EXPLORING DIFFERENT TYPES OF CRYPTOCURRENCIES

The world of cryptocurrency extends far beyond Bitcoin, offering various digital assets, each with its purpose and unique features. Understanding these cryptocurrencies is critical to navigating the ecosystem effectively and tailoring your investment strategy. From the original Bitcoin to the programmable Ethereum and the versatile altcoins like Litecoin and Ripple, each cryptocurrency adds value in its way. Let's look at these major players and their impact on the broader digital economy.

Bitcoin: The Pioneer of Cryptocurrency
Bitcoin remains the most recognizable cryptocurrency and is the foundation upon which the entire industry has been built. Created in 2009 by the pseudonymous Satoshi Nakamoto, Bitcoin introduced the concept of a decentralized digital currency that operates without the oversight of banks or governments. Its launch was revolutionary, coming at a time when the global financial crisis highlighted vulnerabilities in traditional systems.

Bitcoin's essential appeal lies in its simplicity and reliability. It acts as a peer-to-peer electronic cash system, enabling individuals to transfer value securely without intermediaries. Every transaction is recorded on its blockchain, a decentralized ledger that ensures transparency and prevents fraud. To maintain the integrity of the network, Bitcoin employs a proof-of-work mechanism, where miners solve complex mathematical problems to validate transactions and earn rewards in the form of newly minted Bitcoin.

The scarcity of Bitcoin is another aspect that attracts investors. With a cap of 21 million coins, Bitcoin's finite supply makes it akin to digital gold. This characteristic has positioned it as a store of value, especially in times of economic uncertainty. Many investors use Bitcoin as a hedge against inflation, confident in its decentralized nature and resistance to manipulation by central banks.

However, Bitcoin is not without its limitations. Its blockchain can process only a limited number of transactions per second, leading to delays and high fees during periods of high demand. This issue has spurred the development of layer-2 solutions like the Lightning Network, designed to facilitate faster and cheaper transactions. Despite these challenges, Bitcoin remains the dominant cryptocurrency, often seen as the gateway to the world of digital assets.

Ethereum: Programmable Money and Beyond
If Bitcoin is the digital equivalent of gold, Ethereum can be considered the oil fueling an expansive blockchain-based economy. Introduced in 2015 by Vitalik Buterin, Ethereum took blockchain technology to new heights by allowing for programmability. Unlike Bitcoin, which primarily serves as a digital currency, Ethereum's blockchain can host smart contracts—self-executing agreements coded directly into the network.

Smart contracts revolutionized the potential of blockchain. Imagine two strangers agreeing to a transaction, such as a loan, without needing a bank to enforce the terms. With Ethereum, the code enforces the agreement, eliminating intermediaries and reducing costs. This innovation opened the door to Decentralized Finance (DeFi), where services like lending, borrowing, and trading occur entirely on the blockchain.

Ethereum is also the backbone of non-fungible tokens (NFTs). These unique digital assets have gained immense popularity in art, gaming, and collectibles. Platforms like OpenSea, where NFTs are bought and sold, rely on Ethereum's blockchain to authenticate ownership and transfer assets securely.

Despite its versatility, Ethereum faces growing pains. Its network can handle about 15 transactions per second, making it prone to congestion during periods of high demand. Transaction fees and gas fees can skyrocket, discouraging smaller users. To address these issues, Ethereum is transitioning to Ethereum 2.0, an upgrade that will replace its proof-of-work mechanism with proof-of-stake. This shift promises faster transactions, lower fees, and a more environmentally friendly blockchain.

Ethereum's impact on cryptocurrency is profound, offering a platform where innovation thrives. Its adaptability and large developer community ensure its continued relevance as blockchain technology evolves.

Altcoins: Diversity and Innovation
While Bitcoin and Ethereum dominate headlines, thousands of alternative cryptocurrencies—collectively known as altcoins—bring diversity and specialized functionality to the ecosystem. Each altcoin is designed to address specific limitations or introduce new capabilities, enriching the cryptocurrency landscape.

Litecoin, often described as "silver to Bitcoin's gold," was created in 2011 by Charlie Lee to provide faster and cheaper transactions. Its block generation time is significantly shorter than Bitcoin's, allowing quicker transaction processing. This makes Litecoin more suitable for everyday purchases, though it shares Bitcoin's core principles of decentralization and transparency.

Ripple (XRP) takes a different approach, focusing on efficiency in international payments. Unlike Bitcoin and Ethereum, which rely on decentralized mining, Ripple uses a network of trusted validators to quickly and cheaply confirm transactions. This efficiency has attracted partnerships with major financial institutions, making Ripple a leader in cross-border payment solutions. However, it has faced legal and regulatory challenges, particularly in the U.S., impacting its adoption.

Cardano (ADA) represents another innovation in blockchain technology. Founded by Charles Hoskinson, one of Ethereum's co-founders, Cardano emphasizes security, scalability, and sustainability. Its development is guided by peer-reviewed academic research, making it one of the most rigorously tested blockchain platforms. Cardano aims to address Ethereum's scalability issues while maintaining energy efficiency, positioning itself as a strong contender in the smart contract space.

Polkadot (DOT) introduces the concept of interoperability, connecting multiple blockchains to create a unified network. This allows different blockchains to share information and collaborate, paving the way for a more integrated and efficient blockchain ecosystem. Polkadot's vision of interconnected chains has attracted attention from developers and investors alike, highlighting the importance of cross-chain solutions.

Binance Coin (BNB), launched initially as a utility token for the Binance exchange, has grown into a versatile asset with many applications. Beyond reducing trading fees on Binance, BNB powers the Binance Smart Chain, a blockchain designed to support smart contracts and decentralized applications. Its rapid growth and usability make it one of the most valuable altcoins.

Each altcoin offers unique strengths, catering to different needs within the cryptocurrency space. From payment solutions and cross-chain interoperability to energy efficiency and smart contract platforms, these alternatives to Bitcoin and Ethereum demonstrate the breadth of innovation driving the industry forward.

Choosing the Right Cryptocurrency
For a new investor, the sheer variety of cryptocurrencies can be overwhelming. The key is to understand your goals and risk tolerance. Are you looking for a long-term store of value? Bitcoin may be the right choice. Are you interested in participating in the DeFi ecosystem or exploring NFTs? Ethereum could be a better fit. Want faster payments or exposure to emerging blockchain technologies? Altcoins like Litecoin, Cardano, or Polkadot might align with your interests.

It's important to approach cryptocurrency with a sense of curiosity and caution. Each coin has risks and rewards, and the market's volatility requires careful research and thoughtful decision-making. Diversification can also be a powerful strategy, allowing you to spread risk across different projects while exploring their opportunities.

The Expanding Cryptocurrency Landscape
The world of cryptocurrency is constantly evolving, driven by technological innovation and a growing demand for decentralized solutions. From Bitcoin's role as digital gold to Ethereum's transformative smart contracts and the specialized use cases of altcoins, the ecosystem offers something for every investor. By understanding these major cryptocurrencies' unique features and challenges, you'll be better equipped to navigate the digital asset landscape and make informed decisions.

As you continue your journey, the next step is learning to store and manage your cryptocurrency securely. In the following chapter, we'll explore the essential tools and best practices for setting up a wallet, ensuring that your digital assets remain safe as you delve deeper into this exciting new frontier.

Stablecoins and Their Role

Stablecoins stand out as an essential innovation in the cryptocurrency ecosystem, bridging the gap between volatile digital assets and the predictability of traditional financial systems. While Bitcoin and Ethereum often make headlines for their price swings, stablecoins offer a more stable and reliable alternative for various financial activities. Their unique design allows users to harness the advantages of digital currencies while avoiding some risks. This section delves into stablecoins, their diverse mechanisms, and their roles in reshaping how we think about money.

Understanding Stablecoins

To grasp the significance of stablecoins, imagine needing a digital currency for daily transactions that don't fluctuate wildly in value from one hour to the next. Stablecoins address this need by pegging their value to a steady benchmark, such as a fiat currency like the U.S. dollar, a commodity like gold, or even other cryptocurrencies. This stability allows users to conduct transactions confidently, save funds, and access financial services without being at the mercy of unpredictable market swings.

Stablecoins come in three primary types, each employing distinct mechanisms to maintain stability. Fiat-backed stablecoins are the most straightforward, holding reserves of traditional currency equivalent to the amount of digital coins issued. For example, for every Tether (USDT) token in circulation, there is supposed to be one U.S. dollar held in reserve. This one-to-one backing assures users that their stablecoins can always be redeemed for the equivalent fiat currency.

Crypto-collateralized stablecoins take a more decentralized approach, using other cryptocurrencies as collateral instead of fiat currency. Since cryptocurrencies themselves can be volatile, these stablecoins are often over-collateralized. This means the value of the collateral exceeds the value of the stablecoins issued, creating a buffer to absorb price fluctuations in the underlying assets. MakerDAO's DAI is a popular example, relying on a mix of Ethereum and other cryptocurrencies to back its value.

Algorithmic stablecoins, on the other hand, operate without physical or digital collateral. Instead, they use smart contracts to regulate supply and demand. When demand increases, the algorithm creates more coins to stabilize the price. Conversely, it reduces supply during periods of low demand. While innovative, this approach is inherently riskier, as it depends heavily on the effectiveness of the algorithm and market dynamics.

These different stablecoins illustrate blockchain technology's flexibility and ability to offer tailored solutions for stability. They enable users to conduct everyday transactions, save value, or confidently participate in decentralized finance (DeFi) ecosystems.

Popular Stablecoins: How They Differ
Not all stablecoins are created equal, and their nuances matter, especially when choosing which one to use for specific needs. Tether (USDT), USD Coin (USDC), DAI, Binance USD (BUSD), and TrueUSD (TUSD) are among the most widely used stablecoins, each catering to different priorities like transparency, decentralization, or platform integration.

Tether (USDT) is the pioneer of stablecoins, with widespread use and availability across nearly every crypto exchange. Its strength lies in its early adoption and accessibility, making it the go-to choice for traders looking to exit volatile positions quickly. However, Tether has faced significant scrutiny over the years due to its inconsistent reserve transparency. Critics have questioned whether all USDT tokens are fully backed by fiat reserves, raising trust issues among cautious users.

USD Coin (USDC) takes a more transparent approach, prioritizing trust and regulatory compliance. Managed by Circle and Coinbase, USDC undergoes regular audits to ensure its reserves match the amount of stablecoins in circulation. This commitment to accountability has made it a popular choice among institutional users and those prioritizing reliability. Its integration with DeFi platforms further enhances its appeal for earning interest or participating in decentralized ecosystems.

DAI stands out for its decentralized nature, making it a favorite within the DeFi space. Unlike fiat-backed stablecoins, DAI relies on cryptocurrency reserves and smart contracts governed by the MakerDAO community. Its over-collateralization model provides stability while maintaining the ethos of decentralization. However, because volatile assets back it, maintaining its peg requires constant adjustments and a sophisticated understanding of the underlying mechanisms.

Binance USD (BUSD) benefits from its close integration with the Binance ecosystem, one of the largest cryptocurrency exchanges in the world. Issued in partnership with the regulated financial institution Paxos, BUSD combines the reliability of a fiat-backed stablecoin with the convenience of being deeply embedded in Binance's trading and DeFi platforms. For users actively involved in Binance's ecosystem, BUSD offers seamless utility.

TrueUSD (TUSD) also emphasizes transparency and trust, backed by reserves held in third-party trust accounts. Regular audits confirm its backing, appealing to users who value openness in their financial dealings. While less widely used than USDT or USDC, TUSD has gained a reputation for reliability and regulatory compliance.

Each stablecoin offers unique benefits and trade-offs. The right choice depends on your priorities: transparency, decentralization, or integration with specific platforms.

The Pros and Cons of Stablecoins

Stablecoins have undeniably transformed the cryptocurrency landscape, offering significant advantages that address some of the most persistent challenges in digital finance. However, they also come with limitations and risks that users must understand.

One of the most significant advantages of stablecoins is their stability, making them a reliable medium of exchange. For someone like Raj, who works abroad and sends money to his family back home, stablecoins provide a fast, low-cost solution compared to traditional remittance services. Instead of waiting days for a transfer to clear or losing a significant portion to fees, Raj can send stablecoins like USDC instantly, knowing their value will remain consistent.

Beyond remittances, stablecoins are a gateway to decentralized finance. Platforms like Aave and Compound allow users to lend their stablecoins and earn interest, creating opportunities for passive income. For individuals in regions with unstable local currencies, stablecoins offer a secure store of value, shielding them from inflation and economic volatility.

However, stablecoins have their downsides. Centralization risks loom over fiat-backed stablecoins like USDT and USDC. If the issuing entity fails to maintain adequate reserves or faces regulatory challenges, users' confidence in the stablecoin's value could be shaken. Tether's controversies over reserve transparency serve as a cautionary tale, reminding users to scrutinize the entities behind these digital currencies.

Algorithmic stablecoins, while innovative, carry inherent risks due to their reliance on algorithms to maintain value. In extreme market conditions, these mechanisms can fail, leading to a stablecoin price collapse. For instance, some algorithmic stablecoins have experienced "death spirals," where a loss of confidence triggers a cascade of selling, causing the stablecoin to lose its peg entirely.

Another challenge is regulatory uncertainty. Governments worldwide scrutinize stablecoins and are concerned about their potential to disrupt traditional financial systems. While some regulators see stablecoins as a tool for innovation, others view them as a threat, leading to proposals for stricter oversight. This evolving regulatory landscape could impact the availability and use of stablecoins in certain regions.

Despite these risks, stablecoins play a vital role in the cryptocurrency ecosystem. They offer a bridge between the traditional financial world and the decentralized future, enabling users to access digital finance with confidence and convenience.

The Unique Role of Stablecoins
Stablecoins have emerged as a cornerstone of the cryptocurrency market, offering stability and utility in an otherwise volatile space. Their ability to combine the benefits of digital assets with the predictability of fiat currencies makes them indispensable for transactions, savings, and decentralized finance.

For people like Raj or businesses seeking efficient cross-border solutions, stablecoins are more than just a technological innovation—they're a practical tool for real-world financial challenges. However, users must remain vigilant and understand each stablecoin's underlying mechanisms and potential risks.

As the cryptocurrency ecosystem evolves, stablecoins will likely play a critical role in shaping how we interact with money in a digital age. Whether trading on exchanges, participating in DeFi or looking for a stable way to save value, these assets provide a versatile and reliable option. Moving forward, the challenge will be balancing innovation with accountability, ensuring that stablecoins remain functional and trustworthy in the coming years.

Niche Cryptocurrencies and Tokens

The cryptocurrency world is rich with diversity, extending far beyond major players like Bitcoin and Ethereum. It includes a fascinating array of niche cryptocurrencies and tokens, each designed to address unique needs, experiment with innovative ideas, or engage communities in novel ways. From privacy coins that prioritize anonymity to governance tokens that enable collective decision-making, these digital assets showcase the creativity and adaptability of blockchain technology. Understanding these niche assets provides insight into the evolving possibilities of the cryptocurrency ecosystem and how they might align with your goals as an investor or participant.

The Role of Privacy Coins: Confidentiality in a Transparent World

One unique challenge traditional blockchain networks pose is their inherent transparency. While the openness of Bitcoin or Ethereum allows anyone to verify transactions, it can also expose sensitive financial details to public scrutiny. This transparency can be problematic for individuals or businesses that value financial privacy. Privacy coins emerged as a response, leveraging advanced cryptographic techniques to obscure transaction details and provide confidentiality.

Take Monero (XMR), for example. Since its launch in 2014, Monero has been a pioneer in privacy-focused cryptocurrency. Using technologies like ring signatures and stealth addresses, Monero ensures that transaction origins and amounts are hidden. Ring signatures blend a user's transaction with others, creating plausible deniability and making it nearly impossible to trace the funds. Stealth addresses generate one-time use addresses for each transaction, further shielding the sender and receiver's identities. These features have made Monero a favorite among those seeking anonymity, whether for personal security or business confidentiality.

Zcash (ZEC) offers a different take on privacy. Launched in 2016, Zcash introduced zk-SNARKs, a cutting-edge cryptographic method that allows transactions to be verified without revealing any details. Zcash users can choose between shielded transactions, which are private, and transparent transactions, which are visible on the blockchain. This flexibility appeals to users who want privacy options while maintaining the ability to conduct visible, auditable transactions when needed.

However, using privacy coins has sparked debates around their role in potentially illicit activities, such as money laundering. As a result, some exchanges have delisted privacy coins to navigate regulatory concerns. Despite this controversy, privacy coins highlight an ongoing tension in cryptocurrency: the balance between transparency and privacy.

Utility Tokens and Governance Tokens: The Backbone of Blockchain Applications

Blockchain technology has expanded beyond simple value transfer, enabling complex ecosystems of decentralized applications (dApps) and protocols. Within these ecosystems, utility and governance tokens play critical roles in driving functionality and fostering community engagement.

As the name suggests, utility tokens are designed to provide access to specific services within a blockchain platform. Take the Basic Attention Token (BAT), which powers the Brave browser ecosystem. Users earn BAT by opting into privacy-respecting ads, and content creators receive BAT as compensation for their work. This token economy creates a closed-loop system where users and creators interact directly, cutting out traditional advertising intermediaries.

Another notable utility token is Chainlink (LINK), which powers a decentralized oracle network. Chainlink connects blockchain applications to real-world data, enabling smart contracts to execute based on external information like weather updates or stock prices. The LINK token incentivizes data providers to deliver accurate and reliable information, ensuring the network's functionality.

Governance tokens, on the other hand, enable decentralized decision-making within blockchain projects. They grant holders voting rights, allowing them to influence important decisions like protocol updates or fund allocation. This democratized governance model is at the heart of decentralized autonomous organizations (DAOs), which rely on collective participation rather than central control.

Uniswap (UNI) is a prime example of a governance token. As one of the leading decentralized exchanges (DEXs), Uniswap allows UNI holders to vote on protocol changes, such as fee adjustments or liquidity rewards. Similarly, MakerDAO's MKR token empowers its holders to manage the stability of the DAI stablecoin by voting on risk parameters and collateral types.

While these tokens promote decentralization and community involvement, they are not without challenges. Large token holders, often called "whales," can exert disproportionate influence over governance decisions, potentially undermining the democratic ideals of blockchain projects. Despite this, utility and governance tokens represent powerful tools for creating dynamic, user-driven ecosystems.

Meme Coins and Community Coins: Where Fun Meets Finance
In cryptocurrency's playful and sometimes chaotic world, meme coins and community coins have carved out a unique niche. Unlike utility or governance tokens, these coins often need more technical sophistication or specific use cases, instead relying on humor, social trends, and community-driven engagement to generate value.

Dogecoin (DOGE) is the quintessential meme coin. Created in 2013 as a joke based on the Shiba Inu "Doge" meme,

Dogecoin gained an enthusiastic following thanks to its lighthearted branding and accessible design. What started as a playful experiment quickly became a legitimate cryptocurrency with real-world use cases, including tipping content creators online and raising funds for charitable causes. High-profile endorsements, particularly from figures like Elon Musk, further propelled Dogecoin into the mainstream, showcasing the power of community and viral marketing.

Shiba Inu (SHIB) followed in Dogecoin's footsteps, branding itself as the "Dogecoin killer." Launched in 2020, SHIB leveraged a strong social media presence and its community of supporters to achieve remarkable popularity. Like Dogecoin, Shiba Inu thrives on speculation and community-driven hype rather than technical utility.

Community coins, while similar to meme coins in their focus on social engagement, often aim to provide tangible benefits to their users. Rally (RLY), for example, allows creators and influencers to launch their own branded tokens, which can be used to reward fans or grant access to exclusive content. This model fosters more profound connections between creators and their communities, turning fan engagement into a dynamic, tokenized economy.

Meme and community coins illustrate how cryptocurrency can be used for social expression, engagement, and humor. While they often need more technical tokens, their success highlights the importance of community and culture in driving adoption and interest in digital assets.

Balancing Innovation and Practicality

Niche cryptocurrencies and tokens are a testament to the creativity and diversity of the cryptocurrency ecosystem. Privacy coins address fundamental concerns about financial confidentiality, utility tokens power innovative platforms, governance tokens enable decentralized decision-making, and meme coins inject fun and accessibility into the space. Each serves a different audience and purpose, reflecting the multifaceted nature of blockchain technology.

For investors and users, the key is understanding the goals and trade-offs of each token type. Privacy coins may appeal to those prioritizing anonymity but come with regulatory risks. Utility tokens are essential for interacting with specific platforms but may lack broader applicability. Governance tokens empower participation in decentralized projects but can be influenced by large stakeholders. Meme coins may thrive on community enthusiasm but often carry high volatility and speculative risks.

As you explore these niche assets, consider how they align with your goals, values, and risk tolerance whether you're intrigued by the privacy features of Monero, the collaborative potential of governance tokens, or the playful charm of Dogecoin, the cryptocurrency world offers a wide range of opportunities to explore.

Looking Ahead
Niche cryptocurrencies demonstrate the versatility and innovation that define the blockchain space. They challenge traditional financial norms, empower communities, and showcase the diverse ways digital assets can create value. As the cryptocurrency landscape evolves, these tokens will likely play an increasingly important role in shaping the future of decentralized finance, community engagement, and digital expression.

In the next section, we'll explore how to securely store and manage your digital assets, diving into the practicalities of setting up wallets and safeguarding your investments in this dynamic and exciting ecosystem. By understanding the variety of coins and tokens available, you'll be better prepared to navigate the opportunities and challenges of the cryptocurrency world.

CHAPTER 3: SETTING UP YOUR FIRST CRYPTO WALLET

Setting up your first crypto wallet is crucial in your cryptocurrency journey. It's not just a matter of storing digital assets; your wallet represents your gateway to accessing, managing, and securing your investments. Unlike traditional wallets that hold physical cash, a crypto wallet manages your private and public keys, enabling you to interact with the blockchain. Choosing the correct type of wallet is essential to safeguard your assets, as each type offers varying levels of security, convenience, and functionality. Understanding the distinctions between hot and cold wallets will help you make informed decisions based on your needs, whether you're an active trader, a decentralized finance (DeFi) enthusiast, or a long-term investor.

Hot Wallets: Convenience Meets Accessibility
Hot wallets are connected to the internet, making them highly convenient for quick access, transactions, and day-to-day crypto activities. They are trendy among beginners and active traders who need easy access to their funds. However, this convenience comes with a trade-off: hot wallets are inherently more vulnerable to cyber threats.

Mobile wallets are a prime example of hot wallets, offering seamless accessibility through smartphone apps. Imagine carrying a digital bank in your pocket that allows you to pay for a coffee in Bitcoin or interact with decentralized applications (dApps) directly from your phone. Wallets like MetaMask, Trust Wallet, and Mycelium provide user-friendly interfaces and integration with DeFi platforms. While their convenience is unmatched, the challenge lies in ensuring the security of your device. A compromised smartphone can expose your funds, making it crucial to secure your phone with strong passwords and two-factor authentication (2FA).

Desktop wallets, such as Electrum and Exodus, offer another layer of control. Installed on your computer, they provide a secure environment for managing crypto, especially if your computer has robust antivirus software and firewalls. These wallets often include features like portfolio tracking and support for multiple cryptocurrencies. However, they are only as secure as the computer they're on. A malware-infected device could compromise your wallet, so maintaining up-to-date security measures is essential.

Web wallets are the most accessible hot wallets, allowing you to log in from any device with a browser. These wallets are often tied to exchanges like Coinbase or Binance, making them ideal for users who trade frequently. However, because the exchange typically holds the private keys on your behalf, you're entrusting them with significant responsibility. While these platforms invest heavily in security, they remain targets for cyberattacks. For this reason, web wallets should only be used for small amounts of cryptocurrency or short-term needs.

Hot wallets are convenient, making them an excellent choice for users who need quick and frequent access to their funds. However, they're best suited for smaller amounts of crypto due to their exposure to potential online threats.

Cold Wallets: The Gold Standard of Security
Cold wallets are the preferred choice for those prioritizing security above all else. These wallets remain offline, making them immune to hacking attempts and other online risks. They are ideal for long-term storage of significant amounts of cryptocurrency, providing peace of mind for serious investors.

Hardware wallets like Ledger Nano X and Trezor are among

the most popular cold wallets. These physical devices store your private keys offline, protecting your funds even if your computer or smartphone is compromised. Imagine a small, USB-like device that requires physical access to authorize transactions. This additional layer of security makes it nearly impossible for hackers to steal your funds remotely. Hardware wallets do come with a cost, typically ranging from $50 to $200, but their robust protection justifies the investment, particularly for users holding large amounts of crypto.

Paper wallets offer an entirely offline alternative, consisting of a printed document with your private and public keys. While they are free and straightforward to create, they require meticulous care. Think of them as a bearer bond; anyone possessing the paper can access your funds. To protect a paper wallet, store it in a secure location, such as a safe, and consider creating duplicates in case of physical damage or loss. While highly secure against digital threats, paper wallets are less practical for frequent transactions and can be cumbersome to use.

Cold wallets are unparalleled in terms of security, making them the go-to option for "HODLers"—those who plan to hold their crypto assets for extended periods. Their offline nature significantly reduces risks, though they require extra care in handling and storage.

Choosing Between Hot and Cold Wallets
The decision between hot and cold wallets often depends on how you plan to use your cryptocurrency. Suppose you're an active trader or someone who uses crypto for regular transactions. In that case, a hot wallet provides the accessibility you need. For instance, a mobile wallet might be perfect for someone like Jenna, who frequently uses Ethereum to interact with DeFi platforms. She values the ease of connecting her wallet to dApps and making quick trades, even though she understands the importance of securing her phone against potential threats.

On the other hand, if you're like Alex, who has invested in Bitcoin as a long-term store of value, a cold wallet offers the security necessary for peace of mind. Alex uses a hardware wallet to store his private keys, knowing his funds are safe from online attacks. He occasionally connects his wallet to a computer when he needs to make a transaction but keeps it offline securely.

Many users find that a combination of both wallet types works best. For example, Jenna uses a mobile wallet for small, daily transactions. She keeps her long-term holdings in a hardware wallet. This approach allows her to enjoy the convenience of hot wallets while safeguarding the bulk of her assets in cold storage.

Best Practices for Wallet Security
Specific best practices can enhance your security regardless of which wallet you choose. Always back up your wallet by securely storing your seed or recovery phrases. This sequence of words is your lifeline if you lose access to your wallet, so treat it like a master key. Avoid storing your seed phrase digitally, where it could be hacked, and instead, write it down and store it in a safe place.

Enable two-factor authentication (2FA) on your wallet whenever possible. This adds an extra layer of protection, requiring you to verify your identity through a secondary device or app. Use strong, unique passwords for web and mobile wallets and change them regularly. Avoid accessing your wallet on public Wi-Fi networks, exposing you to potential cyber threats.

Be cautious of phishing scams. Never click on unsolicited links or share your private keys or recovery phrase with anyone. Reputable wallet providers and exchanges will never ask for this information. When downloading wallet software, ensure it comes from a verified source to avoid malware or fake applications.

Moving Forward with Confidence

Setting up a crypto wallet is more than a technical step; it's an opportunity to take ownership of your financial future. Whether you're using a hot wallet for convenience or a cold wallet for long-term security, your wallet is your key to accessing the dynamic world of cryptocurrency. By understanding the strengths and limitations of each type, you can choose the option that best aligns with your needs and goals.

As you become more familiar with managing your wallet, you'll gain confidence in handling digital assets. This foundation will prepare you for the next step: learning to set up and secure your wallet correctly. In the following section, we'll provide:

Practical guidance for configuring your first wallet.

Safeguarding your private keys.

Ensuring that your crypto journey begins on solid ground.

With the right tools and knowledge, you'll be ready to navigate the exciting possibilities cryptocurrency offers.

Choosing the Right Wallet for You

Choosing the right cryptocurrency wallet is a deeply personal decision that is vital to securing your digital assets. With many options available, from user-friendly mobile apps to highly secure hardware devices, the decision can feel overwhelming, especially for beginners. The right wallet depends on your unique needs, whether you prioritize security, ease of use, or accessibility. This section will guide you through the critical considerations for selecting a wallet, highlight some of the most popular options, and help you avoid common mistakes that can jeopardize your assets.

Finding the Right Balance Between Security and Usability
The first step in choosing a wallet is understanding the trade-offs between security and usability. If you're new to cryptocurrency, you might feel tempted to choose a wallet solely based on convenience, such as a mobile or web wallet. However, these wallets are connected to the internet, making them more susceptible to cyberattacks like hacking or phishing. On the other hand, hardware wallets, which store your private keys offline, provide unparalleled security but may feel less intuitive and more cumbersome for frequent transactions.

Imagine a scenario where Sarah, a newcomer to cryptocurrency, decides to use a web wallet because it allows her to access her funds anytime, anywhere. While this is great for making small, everyday transactions, Sarah soon realizes she wants to invest a significant amount in Bitcoin for the long term. After learning about the risks of keeping large sums in a hot wallet, she transitions her holdings to a hardware wallet. This way, Sarah balances the convenience of her web wallet for daily use with the robust security of her hardware wallet for long-term storage.

Your choice of wallet should reflect how you plan to use your cryptocurrency. Are you planning to trade actively or hold onto your investment for the future? For active traders, ease of access might outweigh the absolute need for security, but safeguarding assets with a hardware wallet is essential for long-term holders.

Accessibility, Portability, and Asset Compatibility
Another essential factor to consider is how often you'll need access to your crypto and whether your wallet supports the assets you plan to hold. For example, suppose you want to use Ethereum-based decentralized applications (dApps). In that case, a wallet like MetaMask or Trust Wallet is a must, as they are specifically designed to integrate seamlessly with Ethereum and its tokens.

Now consider James, an avid traveler who uses cryptocurrency for cross-border payments. A mobile wallet like Trust Wallet suits his needs perfectly because it allows him to send and receive payments directly from his smartphone, even while moving. However, suppose James will expand his portfolio to include less common cryptocurrencies. In that case, he might look for a wallet like Exodus, which supports various coins and tokens.

When assessing compatibility, ensure your wallet can handle the unique features you need, such as storing non-fungible tokens (NFTs) or staking cryptocurrencies in decentralized finance (DeFi) platforms. Many modern wallets now cater to these needs, but double-checking before committing to a wallet will save you from future headaches.

Comparing Popular Wallets to Fit Your Needs

While there's no one-size-fits-all solution, understanding the strengths and weaknesses of popular wallets can help you narrow down your choices. For instance, if you're a beginner, wallets like Coinbase Wallet and Trust Wallet are great options. Both offer intuitive interfaces and guides to help users navigate their first transactions. Coinbase Wallet even provides integration with the Coinbase exchange, making it easy to buy and manage crypto in one place.

On the other end of the spectrum, hardware wallets like Ledger Nano X and Trezor cater to security-conscious users. By storing private keys offline, these wallets eliminate the risk of online hacking. They're ideal for someone like Maria, a long-term investor who holds significant Bitcoin and wants peace of mind knowing her assets are protected. While hardware wallets involve a financial investment and a steeper learning curve, their security benefits are often worth the effort.

Desktop wallets, such as Exodus, balance accessibility and control. With features like built-in portfolio tracking and support for multiple cryptocurrencies, Exodus is a favorite among users who want a visually appealing and functional wallet. However, since it's connected to the internet, pairing it with solid antivirus software and ensuring regular updates to minimize risks is crucial.

For users deeply immersed in the Ethereum ecosystem, MetaMask offers unparalleled access to dApps and DeFi platforms. As a browser extension and mobile app, MetaMask makes it easy to interact with decentralized exchanges and token swaps. However, because it's a hot wallet, enabling two-factor authentication (2FA) and keeping backup recovery phrases safe is essential.

Each wallet serves a distinct purpose, so it's not uncommon for users to maintain a combination of wallets. For instance, you might use a mobile wallet for daily spending, a browser wallet for DeFi activities, and a hardware wallet to store most of your funds securely.

Avoiding Common Mistakes When Setting Up Your Wallet
As simple as setting up a wallet may seem, it's easy to make mistakes that can have costly consequences. One of the most common errors is failing to back up your wallet properly. Every crypto wallet provides a seed phrase or recovery phrase—a set of words that acts as a master key to restore your wallet if your device is lost, stolen, or damaged. Treat this phrase like a priceless treasure. Write it down on paper (not stored digitally) and keep it in a secure, fireproof location. Losing your seed phrase means losing access to your funds forever.

Another frequent pitfall is over-reliance on hot wallets for large sums of cryptocurrency. While hot wallets are convenient, they are inherently more vulnerable to attacks. Hackers often target exchange-based web wallets, exploiting vulnerabilities to steal funds. If you're holding significant amounts of crypto, move the majority to a hardware wallet, leaving only what you need for daily transactions in your hot wallet.

Additionally, be cautious about phishing scams. Scammers frequently impersonate wallet providers, sending emails or messages that appear legitimate but are designed to steal your private keys or seed phrases. Always verify the source of any communication and avoid clicking on unsolicited links.

Neglecting basic security practices is another mistake to avoid. For example, failing to enable 2FA or using weak passwords can leave your wallet exposed. Make it a habit to use strong, unique passwords for your wallet and allows every security feature available. Also, keep your wallet software updated to protect against the latest vulnerabilities.

Finally, please don't rush into downloading wallet apps or extensions without verifying their legitimacy. Stick to well-known and reputable wallets, downloading them only from official websites or app stores. Fake apps designed to mimic popular wallets can easily trick users into revealing their private information.

Crafting Your Wallet Strategy
Choosing the right wallet is a decision that evolves with your cryptocurrency journey. As you gain experience, your needs may change, and your wallet strategy should adapt accordingly. Many users find diversifying their wallets based on their specific use cases helpful. For instance, you might use a mobile wallet for quick access and transactions, a browser wallet for DeFi exploration, and a hardware wallet for long-term storage.

Think of your wallets as tools in a toolbox. Each has its strengths and limitations, but they provide comprehensive security and functionality when used together strategically. Start by assessing your immediate needs—are you planning to trade frequently, or are you investing for the long term? As your portfolio grows, consider whether you need additional wallets to handle new types of assets or activities.

With the proper wallet setup, you'll be well-equipped to manage your cryptocurrency confidently. In the next section, we'll guide you through the practical steps of setting up and securing your first wallet, ensuring that you're ready to take complete control of your digital assets. Whether you're a beginner dipping your toes into the crypto world or a seasoned investor, a well-chosen wallet is your key to navigating the exciting possibilities of blockchain technology safely and effectively.

Setting Up and Securing Your Wallet
Setting up and securing your cryptocurrency wallet is a foundational step in your journey into the crypto world. A wallet doesn't hold cryptocurrency directly—it manages the private keys that allow you to access and control your digital assets stored on the blockchain. Securing these keys is critical because any compromise can result in irreversible loss. Let's dive into the practical process of setting up your wallet, explore the best practices to keep it secure, and understand the key features that protect your funds.

Getting Started: Setting Up Your Wallet
The setup process for a crypto wallet depends on whether you're using a hot wallet (mobile, desktop, or web) or a cold wallet (hardware or paper). Each type serves different purposes and comes with unique steps.

For hot wallets, the process is straightforward. Start by selecting a reputable wallet app like Trust Wallet or Exodus. Download the app only from official sources like verified app stores or the provider's website to avoid malware. Once installed, follow the prompts to create a new wallet. This step generates a unique wallet address along with a private key. This critical information grants you control over your funds.

As part of the setup, you'll receive a recovery phrase of 12 to 24 words. This phrase is your safety net, allowing you to restore your wallet if your device is lost or damaged. Write it down carefully and store it securely—don't save it digitally to minimize exposure to hacking. Many wallets will ask you to verify the recovery phrase to ensure you've recorded it correctly.

The process involves a few additional steps for cold wallets, such as hardware devices like Ledger or Trezor. Start by purchasing your device directly from the manufacturer to ensure it hasn't been tampered with. Upon receiving it, set up the wallet using the companion software, such as Ledger Live. The device will generate a recovery phrase that you must store securely, and you'll set up a PIN code to prevent unauthorized access. Once your wallet is configured, you can transfer cryptocurrency from exchanges or other wallets to your cold storage for safekeeping.

Securing Your Wallet: Best Practices
Setting up your wallet is only half the battle; securing it is equally, if not more, important. Your approach to security begins with strong passwords and safe management of your recovery phrase.

A strong password is your first defense, especially for hot wallets. Avoid using easily guessed combinations like birthdays or common words. Instead, create a unique password with a mix of uppercase and lowercase letters, numbers, and symbols. If you find it challenging to manage multiple complex passwords, consider using a trusted password manager.

Your recovery phrase is your ultimate failsafe. Treat it like the keys to a vault. Please write it down on paper and store it in a safe place, such as a fireproof or waterproof safe. Some users go a step further by engraving the phrase on a metal sheet to protect it from fire or physical damage. Never share your recovery phrase with anyone—not even technical support representatives—and avoid storing it digitally, as this exposes it to potential hacks or phishing attacks.

Two-factor authentication (2FA) adds a layer of security for hot wallets. Requiring a secondary verification step—often from an authenticator app—makes it significantly harder for unauthorized users to access your wallet, even if they have your password. Avoid using SMS-based 2FA when possible, as it is more vulnerable to SIM-swapping attacks.

Redundancy is vital when safeguarding your recovery phase. Consider creating multiple paper copies and storing them in different secure locations. This ensures you retain access to your funds even if one copy is lost or damaged. Always keep these copies in separate locations to minimize risk from events like fires or theft.

Understanding Wallet Security Features
Crypto wallets come equipped with various security features designed to protect your assets. Familiarizing yourself with these tools can help you build a robust defense against potential threats.

Two-factor authentication is a staple for many hot wallets, ensuring that an attacker still needs access to your authenticator app even if your password is compromised. Some wallets, especially mobile ones, also include biometric security options, such as fingerprint or facial recognition. These features add convenience while enhancing protection.

Hardware wallets, known for their strong security, rely on a PIN code to prevent unauthorized access. Many devices also include a self-destruct feature, where multiple incorrect PIN attempts will wipe the wallet clean, preserving your funds as long as you have your recovery phrase.

Multi-signature (multi-sig) wallets add another layer of security by requiring multiple keys to authorize a transaction. For example, a multi-sig wallet might require three out of five possible keys to sign off on a transaction. This setup benefits shared accounts or users who want to distribute access across multiple devices.

Address whitelisting is another useful feature offered by some wallets and exchanges. This allows you to pre-approve certain wallet addresses for withdrawals, ensuring that funds can only be sent to trusted addresses even if your account is compromised. Similarly, setting withdrawal limits can restrict the amount of cryptocurrency that can be moved within a specific time frame, adding another safeguard.

Regular software updates are critical for maintaining wallet security. Wallet providers frequently release updates to fix vulnerabilities, patch bugs, and introduce new features. Always download updates directly from official sources to avoid counterfeit software that could compromise your wallet.

Practical Advice for Ongoing Security

Even with robust wallet security features, vigilance is critical. The cryptocurrency space is rife with scams and phishing attempts. Be cautious of unsolicited emails or messages claiming to be from your wallet provider or exchange. These often include links to fake websites designed to steal your private keys or recovery phrases. Always double-check URLs and access your wallet only through verified channels.

Avoid public Wi-Fi when accessing your wallet, especially for transactions. Public networks are more vulnerable to interception, putting your private information at risk. If you must use public Wi-Fi, consider using a virtual private network (VPN) to encrypt your connection.

Diversifying your wallet strategy can also enhance security. For example, keep a small amount of cryptocurrency in a hot wallet for daily transactions and store the majority in a cold wallet. This way, even if your hot wallet is compromised, the impact on your holdings will be minimal.

Building Confidence Through Practice

Setting up and securing a crypto wallet may seem intimidating at first. Still, with careful attention to detail, it becomes a straightforward process. For instance, imagine Alex, a beginner who set up his first wallet. Initially, he felt overwhelmed by the need to secure his recovery phrase and enable two-factor authentication. However, he gained confidence in managing his wallet by following best practices and taking it step by step. Now, Alex feels empowered, knowing his funds are protected and under his complete control.

As you gain experience, managing your wallet will become second nature. Take the time to familiarize yourself with its features, practice sending and receiving small amounts of cryptocurrency, and regularly review your security settings. This proactive approach will help you avoid potential threats and ensure your assets remain safe.

The Foundation of Your Crypto Journey
Your crypto wallet is the cornerstone of your cryptocurrency journey, acting as a gateway and a safeguard for your assets. Setting up your wallet thoughtfully and prioritizing security lays the groundwork for confident participation in the crypto ecosystem. Whether you're using a hot wallet for convenience or a cold wallet for long-term storage, understanding how to protect your private keys and recovery phrases is essential.

As you move forward, remember that your wallet's security is ultimately in your hands. Stay informed, follow best practices, and adapt to new security measures as they emerge. With a well-secured wallet, you can explore the exciting opportunities of cryptocurrency with peace of mind, knowing your assets are protected. In the next chapter, we'll guide you through making your first cryptocurrency purchase, building on the solid foundation of wallet security you've now established. Let's take the next step in your crypto journey together.

CHAPTER 4: GETTING STARTED ON CRYPTO EXCHANGES

Understanding how to use cryptocurrency exchanges is one of the most important steps in your journey into the digital asset space. Exchanges are the gateways to buying, selling, and trading cryptocurrencies, but not all exchanges function the same way. Broadly, exchanges are divided into two main types: centralized exchanges (CEXs) and decentralized exchanges (DEXs). Each type has its unique advantages and challenges, and the choice between them often depends on your goals, preferences, and level of experience.

Centralized Exchanges: Convenience and Structure

Centralized exchanges (CEXs) are the most common and beginner-friendly platforms for trading cryptocurrency. Managed by centralized companies, these platforms act as intermediaries that facilitate transactions between buyers and sellers. Think of them like traditional stock exchanges but for digital assets. Platforms like Binance, Coinbase, and Kraken are examples of CEXs that have become household names in the crypto world.

The ease of use offered by CEXs is one of their most significant advantages. For instance, if you're completely new to crypto, you can sign up for a platform like Coinbase in just a few minutes, deposit fiat currency (like dollars or euros), and start buying Bitcoin, Ethereum, or other cryptocurrencies almost immediately. The user interfaces are designed to be intuitive, with features like real-time charts, price tracking, and simple buy/sell buttons. This accessibility makes CEXs an excellent starting point for beginners.

However, CEXs operate on a custodial model, meaning that when you deposit funds, the exchange holds custody of your assets. This structure simplifies the trading experience but comes with risks. By entrusting your funds to the exchange, you are dependent on its security measures. While major platforms invest heavily in protecting user funds, history has shown that no centralized platform is immune to hacking or mismanagement. The infamous Mt. Gox hack, for example, resulted in the loss of over 850,000 Bitcoin, highlighting the potential risks.

CEXs offer a wealth of tools for users seeking advanced trading features. From stop-loss orders to margin trading and futures contracts, these platforms cater to experienced traders looking to employ sophisticated strategies. Liquidity is another strength of CEXs, as their large user bases ensure faster order execution and less price fluctuation, especially for major cryptocurrencies.

Decentralized Exchanges: Control and Privacy
In contrast to CEXs, decentralized exchanges (DEXs) offer a fundamentally different experience. Instead of being managed by a centralized company, DEXs are built on blockchain technology and operate through self-executing smart contracts. This decentralized model eliminates the need for intermediaries, allowing users to trade directly with one another.

When using a DEX like Uniswap, PancakeSwap, or SushiSwap, you remain in control of your assets at all times. There's no need to deposit funds into the platform, as trades are executed directly from your personal crypto wallet. This self-custody approach aligns with the core ethos of cryptocurrency—giving individuals full control over their funds without relying on third parties.

Privacy is another compelling advantage of DEXs. Most platforms do not require Know Your Customer (KYC) verification, meaning you can trade without providing personal information. For privacy-conscious users or those in regions with strict financial regulations, DEXs provide a way to access the crypto market without sacrificing anonymity.

However, using a DEX requires a higher level of technical knowledge. Unlike the straightforward onboarding process of CEXs, DEXs require you to connect a compatible crypto wallet, such as MetaMask, to interact with the platform. You'll also need to understand concepts like liquidity pools and gas fees, which can be daunting for newcomers.

Liquidity is another challenge for DEXs. While major platforms like Uniswap have significant trading volumes, smaller DEXs may struggle with liquidity, leading to slower transactions and higher price slippage. Additionally, DEXs generally do not support fiat currencies, so you'll need to already own cryptocurrency to get started.

Deciding Between CEXs and DEXs
Choosing between a centralized exchange and a decentralized exchange often depends on your priorities. If you value convenience, user-friendly interfaces, and the ability to buy cryptocurrency directly with fiat currency, a CEX is likely the best fit. These platforms are particularly beneficial for beginners or those making large trades, as they offer robust liquidity and advanced trading tools.

On the other hand, if maintaining control over your assets and privacy are your top priorities, a DEX might be more appealing. For instance, consider a trader like Lisa, who values financial independence and wants to avoid entrusting her funds to a third party. By using a DEX, Lisa retains full custody of her assets, allowing her to trade securely from her wallet while enjoying greater privacy.

Experienced crypto users often leverage both types of exchanges. For example, Alex uses Binance, a CEX, to convert fiat into cryptocurrency because of its ease of use and fiat on-ramp. He then transfers some of his funds to a DEX like Uniswap to explore decentralized finance (DeFi) opportunities and enjoy the self-custody benefits.

Evaluating the Pros and Cons
Both CEXs and DEXs have their strengths and weaknesses. For example, the structured environment of CEXs offers features like 24/7 customer support, fiat on-ramps, and advanced trading tools. However, the trade-off is reduced privacy and the need to trust the platform's security measures.

DEXs, by contrast, empower users with full control over their funds and greater anonymity. However, these benefits come with challenges like lower liquidity, higher fees during network congestion, and a steeper learning curve. For someone like John, who prioritizes security and privacy, a DEX provides peace of mind, even if the trading process is less streamlined.

Avoiding Pitfalls and Enhancing Your Exchange Experience
Regardless of the type of exchange you choose, there are common pitfalls to avoid. Always prioritize security by enabling two-factor authentication (2FA) on your CEX account or safeguarding the private keys of your DEX wallet. Be cautious about phishing attempts, as scammers often impersonate exchanges to steal login credentials or private keys.

For CEX users, withdraw your funds to a personal wallet when not actively trading. Keeping assets on an exchange exposes them to potential risks, such as hacking or insolvency. Remember, "not your keys, not your coins"—a phrase that emphasizes the importance of self-custody in the crypto world.

DEX users should be mindful of transaction fees, especially on networks like Ethereum, where gas fees can spike during periods of high demand. Plan your trades strategically to minimize costs, and consider using layer-2 solutions or alternative blockchains with lower fees.

Charting Your Path in Crypto Trading

Crypto exchanges open the door to the dynamic digital economy, offering you the tools to buy, sell, and trade cryptocurrencies. Whether you're drawn to the user-friendly convenience of a centralized exchange (CEX) or the autonomy and privacy of a decentralized exchange (DEX), understanding these platforms is key to navigating the crypto market with confidence. Take the time to evaluate your priorities, weigh the advantages of each, and begin with small, calculated trades to build your expertise.

As you gain familiarity with trading, you'll discover a strategy that aligns with your goals, blending the strengths of both CEXs and DEXs to optimize your experience. In the next section, we'll guide you step-by-step through setting up your first exchange account and connecting your wallet to a DEX. With these skills, you'll be equipped to trade securely, confidently, and effectively as you embark on your cryptocurrency journey.

Setting Up and Using Your Exchange Account

Setting up and using a cryptocurrency exchange account is an important first step in your crypto journey. While the process might seem daunting at first, a careful, methodical approach can ensure both ease and security. This section will walk you through the steps of creating and verifying your account, linking a payment method, and implementing best practices to protect your assets, all while emphasizing practical advice to help you feel confident and in control.

Creating and Verifying an Account

Starting your crypto journey begins with creating an account on a trusted cryptocurrency exchange. Each platform has a slightly different setup process, but the general steps are similar across the board. First, always ensure you're visiting the correct website. Fraudulent phishing sites are a common threat in the crypto space. For example, if you're setting up an account on Binance or Coinbase, double-check the URL and bookmark it for future use. This small precaution can prevent unnecessary headaches later.

After accessing the official website, click on the registration button and fill in the required details. Typically, you'll need to provide an email address and create a secure password. Your password is your first line of defense, so choose something unique and complex—combine upper and lowercase letters, numbers, and special characters. Avoid the temptation to reuse passwords from other accounts; a compromised password elsewhere could put your crypto holdings at risk.

Once you've completed the initial registration, you'll receive an email verification link. This step ensures your email address is valid and that you can access critical notifications from the exchange. Click the link promptly to confirm your account.

Many exchanges, especially those offering fiat currency transactions, require identity verification through a process called Know Your Customer (KYC). While this step might feel intrusive, it's essential for regulatory compliance and helps establish trust in the platform. Typically, KYC involves uploading a government-issued ID, such as a passport or driver's license, and sometimes a selfie to confirm your identity. Some exchanges may also request proof of address, like a utility bill. While the verification process might take anywhere from a few minutes to several days, it's worth the wait for increased account security and higher trading limits.

After your account is verified, don't forget to enable two-factor authentication (2FA). This added layer of security requires you to enter a time-sensitive code generated by an authenticator app each time you log in or make a transaction. It's one of the simplest yet most effective ways to secure your account.

Linking Your Bank Account or Payment Method

Funding your exchange account is the next step toward making your first cryptocurrency purchase. The best payment method for you depends on your priorities—whether that's minimizing fees, speeding up transactions, or avoiding certain banking restrictions.

Most exchanges have a section dedicated to payments or funding. Start by navigating to this area and selecting the option to add a payment method. If you're planning to use a bank account, prepare to provide your bank's routing and account numbers. Many exchanges perform a verification step for bank accounts, such as sending small test deposits. You'll need to log in to your bank account and confirm these amounts on the exchange to complete the linkage. Bank transfers are a cost-effective option for depositing large amounts, though they may take a day or two to process.

If you prefer faster funding, using a credit or debit card might be a better option. Exchanges like Coinbase make this process straightforward, asking you to enter your card details and verify them with a small authorization charge. While card payments are nearly instant, they often come with higher fees compared to bank transfers. Additionally, some banks may block crypto-related transactions, so it's wise to check with your bank beforehand or consider using a prepaid card as an alternative.

In regions where other payment options like PayPal, Apple Pay, or Google Pay are supported, these methods can offer added convenience. However, these options may not always allow direct crypto withdrawals, so ensure the method aligns with your trading goals.

Once your payment method is linked, deposit funds into your exchange account. Many exchanges let you choose the amount and currency you wish to deposit, and the funds will typically appear in your account once the transaction clears. This balance becomes your buying power for cryptocurrencies.

Best Practices for Account Security
Security is paramount in the cryptocurrency world. As crypto ownership becomes more mainstream, exchanges have become increasingly robust in their security measures, but individual account vulnerabilities remain a common entry point for hackers. Following best practices can help safeguard your funds.

Two-factor authentication (2FA) should be non-negotiable for any crypto trader. While many exchanges default to SMS-based 2FA, app-based options like Google Authenticator or Authy are far more secure. With app-based 2FA, even if someone gains access to your phone number through a SIM-swapping attack, they still can't access your account without the unique codes generated by the app.

Your password is another critical component of your account's security. A strong password isn't just a mix of characters; it's also unique. Reusing a password from another platform can expose your account if that platform is compromised. Consider using a reputable password manager to generate and store complex passwords.

Phishing scams are another prevalent threat. Always approach unsolicited emails, texts, or direct messages claiming to be from your exchange with caution. Double-check URLs before clicking on links, and never enter your credentials on a site unless you're certain it's legitimate. Bookmarking the official exchange website can save you from accidental visits to phishing sites.

Monitoring your account activity regularly is another proactive measure. Most exchanges provide a log of recent actions, including logins, withdrawals, and trades. By reviewing this activity, you can quickly spot unauthorized actions and alert the exchange's support team if needed. Many platforms also allow you to set up account alerts for unusual activity, giving you an added layer of oversight.

For those holding significant amounts of cryptocurrency, enabling withdrawal whitelists can be a lifesaver. This feature ensures that funds can only be withdrawn to pre-approved wallet addresses. Even if your account is compromised, the attacker won't be able to redirect your funds elsewhere.

Finally, consider the broader context of your account security. Are you using a secure device to access your exchange? Is your operating system up to date? Does your device have reliable antivirus software? Small steps like these can close vulnerabilities that hackers often exploit.

Building Confidence in Your Setup
Creating, funding, and securing your exchange account lays the foundation for your cryptocurrency trading journey. While the steps might seem tedious initially, each one contributes to the overall security of your assets and ensures a smoother experience down the road.

Take time to familiarize yourself with the exchange's interface. Whether it's understanding how to view your balance, initiate a trade, or withdraw funds, practice navigating the platform before making significant transactions. If you ever feel overwhelmed, many exchanges offer tutorials, customer support, or community forums where you can ask questions and seek guidance.

As you progress, consider starting with smaller deposits and trades to build confidence. This hands-on approach allows you to learn the mechanics of trading without risking substantial funds. With time and experience, you'll develop the skills needed to navigate the exchange efficiently and make informed decisions about your investments.

Setting up and using an exchange account is about more than accessing the crypto market—it's about laying the groundwork for a secure, confident, and informed trading journey. By taking the time to understand each step, from creating an account to linking a payment method and securing your assets, you're equipping yourself to navigate the dynamic world of cryptocurrency with ease. In the next chapter, we'll explore the exciting process of making your first crypto purchase, turning your setup into action, and beginning your journey as a crypto investor.

CHAPTER 5: MAKING YOUR FIRST CRYPTO PURCHASE

Making your first cryptocurrency purchase is a milestone in your journey into the digital asset world. This step involves acquiring crypto, understanding the market dynamics, and ensuring your choices align with your financial goals. This chapter will prepare you to make your first purchase by exploring key concepts such as market and limit orders, selecting the right cryptocurrency, and setting a realistic budget. These foundational elements will empower you to approach the crypto market with confidence and clarity.

Understanding Market Orders vs. Limit Orders

When you're ready to buy cryptocurrency, the type of order you choose can significantly impact your trading experience. Market and limit orders are the two primary methods used on exchanges, each suited to different needs and strategies.

Market orders are the most straightforward way to make a purchase. When you place a market order, the exchange executes the transaction at the best price. This immediacy makes market orders ideal for beginners who want to acquire cryptocurrency quickly without delving into complex pricing strategies.

However, while market orders are convenient, they come with trade-offs. Since you're buying at the current market price, you have little control over the final execution price. This is particularly relevant in highly volatile markets where prices can shift rapidly within seconds. For example, if the price of Bitcoin is fluctuating sharply, your market order might be executed at a slightly higher price than you anticipated. This effect, known as "slippage," is especially pronounced in low-liquidity markets where fewer buy and sell orders are available.

Limit orders, however, give you more control over your price. When placing a limit order, specify the maximum price you will pay for a cryptocurrency. The order will only be executed if the market price matches or falls below your specified price. This level of precision benefits those who want to avoid overpaying or who aim to buy during a price dip.

However, limit orders come with their own set of challenges. Unlike market orders, which execute instantly, limit orders remain open until the market hits your desired price point. Depending on market conditions, this could take minutes, hours, or even days. This delay might feel frustrating for beginners, but it's a useful strategy for those who want to manage costs effectively.

Market orders are often the best choice for your first purchase because of their simplicity and speed. Once you've gained experience and confidence, experimenting with limit orders can add more depth and control to your trading strategy.

Choosing the Right Cryptocurrency for Your First Purchase
The world of cryptocurrency is vast and diverse, with thousands of coins and tokens. This abundance can be overwhelming for a beginner, but a few practical steps can simplify your decision-making process.

Starting with well-established cryptocurrencies is often the safest route. Bitcoin (BTC) and Ethereum (ETH) are popular for first-time buyers because of their widespread adoption, strong track records, and relatively lower volatility than smaller, less established coins. Bitcoin, often called "digital gold," is widely seen as a store of value, while Ethereum offers a unique ecosystem for decentralized applications and smart contracts.

Another important factor to consider is market capitalization.

Cryptocurrencies with larger market caps, like Bitcoin and Ethereum, tend to have more liquidity and stability. In contrast, smaller-cap coins, often called altcoins, can offer higher potential returns but come with significantly higher risk. For a beginner, focusing on larger-cap assets is a safer way to start, while altcoins can be explored later as you gain more experience.

Understanding the purpose and utility of a cryptocurrency is also critical. Research the project behind the coin, its use case, and its development team. For example, Ethereum's ability to host decentralized applications (dApps) and enable decentralized finance (DeFi) gives it a unique value proposition. Coins with a clear, practical use case often have more substantial long-term potential than those driven solely by speculation.

Finally, consider the coin's liquidity. Highly liquid assets are easier to buy and sell without affecting market price. Bitcoin and Ethereum, being the most traded cryptocurrencies, are generally more liquid than smaller coins, making them a practical choice for your first purchase.

Setting a Realistic Budget
Deciding how much to invest in cryptocurrency is one of the most critical steps in managing your risk. Cryptocurrency markets are volatile, with prices that can soar or plummet within hours. Setting a clear and realistic budget helps you avoid overextending yourself financially and keeps your investments aligned with your long-term goals.

The golden rule of investing in cryptocurrency is only to invest what you can afford to lose. This principle acknowledges the inherent risks of the market and ensures that potential losses won't jeopardize your financial well-being. Avoid using borrowed money or funds earmarked for essential expenses, like rent or emergency savings.

Starting small is another practical approach for beginners. Making a modest initial investment allows you to familiarize yourself with the market without taking on significant risk. For example, you might begin with a small amount, such as $50 or $100, to gain hands-on experience buying, holding, and tracking a cryptocurrency.

Some investors allocate a specific percentage of their overall portfolio to cryptocurrency. For example, you might dedicate 5% of your investment portfolio to digital assets, with the remaining 95% allocated to more traditional investments like stocks or bonds. This strategy provides exposure to the high-growth potential of cryptocurrency while maintaining a diversified and balanced portfolio.

A particularly effective strategy for beginners is dollar-cost averaging (DCA). This involves investing a fixed amount of money at regular intervals, regardless of the asset's price. By spreading your investments over time, you reduce the impact of short-term price volatility and avoid the pressure of trying to time the market. For instance, you might commit to investing $50 per month in Bitcoin, steadily building your holdings over time.

Finally, be mindful of transaction fees when setting your budget. Most exchanges charge fees for buying and selling cryptocurrency, ranging from a flat fee to a percentage of the transaction amount. Understanding these fees and factoring them into your budget ensures that you're aware of the situation.

Building Confidence in Your First Purchase
Understanding market dynamics, selecting the right cryptocurrency, and setting a thoughtful budget lays a solid foundation for your first purchase. With these preparations, you can take the next step and make your first trade.

Start by logging into your chosen exchange and navigating to the trading interface. Select the cryptocurrency you want to purchase and choose whether to place a market order for instant execution or a limit order for greater price control. Enter the amount you wish to invest and review the transaction details carefully before confirming.

Once your purchase is complete, your newly acquired cryptocurrency will appear in your exchange wallet. For beginners, keeping your funds in the exchange wallet is convenient, but as you grow more comfortable, consider transferring your assets to a personal wallet for added security.

Remember, your first cryptocurrency purchase is just the beginning of your journey. Take the time to monitor your investment, track market trends, and continue building your knowledge. The experience you gain will improve your understanding of the crypto market and prepare you for more advanced strategies in the future.

By approaching your first purchase with careful preparation and a clear plan, you can confidently navigate the process and make informed decisions that align with your goals. In the next section, we'll guide you through tracking your investment and managing your portfolio, ensuring your crypto journey remains steady and secure.

Executing the Purchase
Executing your first cryptocurrency purchase is an exciting and rewarding step in your journey toward understanding and investing in digital assets. However, it involves more than simply clicking "buy." Each part of the process—from initiating the purchase to storing your assets securely—requires careful attention to ensure a smooth experience and safeguard your investment. In this chapter, we'll guide you through making your first crypto purchase, monitoring the transaction, and securing your newly acquired assets.

Step-by-Step Guide to Buying Cryptocurrency

Making your first cryptocurrency purchase is straightforward when you follow a clear process. Whether you're using a centralized exchange (CEX) or a decentralized exchange (DEX), the steps are generally similar and user-friendly for beginners.

Start by logging into the exchange account you've already set up. Always double-check that you're on the official exchange website or mobile app to avoid phishing scams. Ensuring a secure connection, such as using a private Wi-Fi network, adds protection.

Once logged in, navigate to the trading section, often labeled as "Buy/Sell" or "Trade." Here, you'll find options to buy various cryptocurrencies using fiat currency or other crypto assets. If you need clarification on the cryptocurrency ticker symbols (e.g., BTC for Bitcoin, ETH for Ethereum), most platforms include a search function to help you locate the asset you want to purchase.

Select the type of order that best suits your needs. A market order is typically the easiest option for beginners, allowing you to purchase cryptocurrency at the current market price without worrying about setting specific price points. If you're more price-conscious and willing to wait, consider placing a limit order to buy only when the price reaches your desired level.

Enter the amount you want to invest. Most exchanges let you specify the amount in your local currency, such as $100 worth of Bitcoin, or in cryptocurrency terms, such as 0.002 BTC. Double-check all details before confirming, as crypto transactions are irreversible.

After confirming your purchase, the exchange processes the order. If you're using two-factor authentication (2FA), you'll be prompted to verify the transaction with a time-sensitive code from your authenticator app. Once completed, your cryptocurrency will appear in your exchange wallet. This process is usually quick, but processing times may vary depending on market activity and the cryptocurrency network.

Monitoring Transaction Confirmation
When you buy cryptocurrency, especially on a blockchain-based platform, it's essential to understand how transaction confirmations work. These confirmations are part of the blockchain's security mechanism and ensure the authenticity of your transaction.

Confirmations occur as new blocks are added to the blockchain, validating and securing your transaction. For example, Bitcoin transactions are typically considered secure after six confirmations, while Ethereum may require around 12. Each confirmation adds another layer of trust, reducing the likelihood of fraud or double-spending.

Most exchanges provide a transaction history section where you can view the status of your purchase. It may show as "Pending," "Processing," or "Completed." This indicates whether the exchange is still verifying the transaction or awaiting blockchain confirmations.

To monitor confirmations more closely, use a blockchain explorer. These tools, such as blockchain.com for Bitcoin or etherscan.io for Ethereum, allow you to track your transactions in real time. Copy the transaction ID (TXID) from your exchange account and paste it into the explorer's search bar. This lets you see the number of confirmations, transaction fees, and the block in which your transaction is recorded.

It's normal for confirmations to take a few minutes to several hours, depending on the blockchain's congestion and transaction fees. Patience is key, as network delays are common during peak trading times.

Storing and Securing Your Purchase

After your cryptocurrency purchase, the next critical step is ensuring your assets are secure. While exchange wallets are convenient for active trading, there are better options for long-term storage. Transferring your funds to a personal wallet gives you full control and reduces the risk of losing assets due to exchange hacks or other vulnerabilities.

Start by choosing the type of wallet that aligns with your needs. A hot wallet like Trust Wallet (mobile) or Exodus (desktop) is a convenient option for smaller amounts or frequent trading. These wallets are connected to the internet, making them accessible but more vulnerable to cyberattacks. For larger holdings or long-term investments, a hardware wallet like Ledger or Trezor offers unmatched security by keeping your private keys offline.

First, to transfer funds from the exchange to your personal wallet, copy your wallet address from the wallet application. Be meticulous here—crypto transactions are irreversible, and sending funds to the wrong address means they're lost forever. Paste the address into the exchange's withdrawal section and specify the amount you want to transfer. Confirm the transaction details, including any withdrawal fees, before proceeding.

Once the transaction is processed, your funds will appear in your wallet. Like purchases, withdrawals also require confirmations on the blockchain, so use a blockchain explorer to monitor the transfer if needed.

Securing your wallet is just as important as transferring your funds. Upon setting up your personal wallet, you'll receive a recovery phrase—a series of 12 to 24 words that act as a backup for your wallet. Write this phrase down on paper and store it in a safe, secure location, such as a fireproof safe. Never store your recovery phrase digitally, exposing it to potential hacking.

For added security, enable two-factor authentication (2FA) on your wallet if supported. This extra step ensures that even if someone gains access to your device, they cannot open your wallet without the authentication code.

Hardware wallets are the gold standard for securing cryptocurrency. These offline devices store your private keys securely, preventing unauthorized access even if your computer or phone is compromised. Investing in a hardware wallet is smart if you plan to hold significant amounts of cryptocurrency long-term.

Navigating Post-Purchase Considerations
Owning cryptocurrency involves more than buying and storing—it's also about managing your holdings and staying informed about the market. Regularly check your wallet balance and transaction history to ensure everything is as expected. Many wallets also offer portfolio tracking features, allowing you to monitor the value of your assets in real-time.

Be cautious about sharing any details related to your cryptocurrency. Scammers often target crypto users by posing as support agents or exchange representatives, asking for private keys or recovery phrases. Remember, no legitimate platform will ever ask for this information.

If you're using a personal wallet, consider diversifying your storage methods. For example, keep a small amount in a mobile wallet for everyday transactions and the majority in a hardware wallet for long-term security. This balance provides both convenience and safety.

Finally, educate yourself continually. The cryptocurrency market evolves rapidly, with new projects, technologies, and regulations constantly emerging. Staying informed helps you make better decisions and protects you from potential risks.

Making your first cryptocurrency purchase is an important milestone that requires careful execution and attention to detail. By following a structured approach—choosing the right order type, monitoring transaction confirmations, and securing your assets in a personal wallet—you can confidently enter the world of digital assets. This process protects your investment and sets the stage for a successful and informed journey into cryptocurrency. As you move forward, focus on building your knowledge and refining your strategies to effectively navigate this dynamic and exciting market. The next chapter'll explore advanced tools and techniques for managing and diversifying your crypto portfolio.

Tracking Your Investment
Tracking your cryptocurrency investments is essential to managing and optimizing your portfolio. Once you've made your first purchase, the next step is to develop habits and strategies that keep you informed and prepared for market changes. Cryptocurrency markets are highly volatile, with prices influenced by a variety of factors. By leveraging tools and understanding the nuances of the market, you can make informed decisions, reduce stress, and maximize the potential of your investments.

Using Apps to Track Your Portfolio
Tracking your portfolio is key to staying organized and understanding the performance of your investments. Thankfully, a range of tools is available to help you monitor your assets efficiently, from beginner-friendly platforms to advanced applications for seasoned investors.

For a simple and accessible approach, platforms like CoinMarketCap and CoinGecko are excellent starting points. These websites and apps provide real-time price updates for thousands of cryptocurrencies, allowing you to input the amount of each asset you hold. This automatically calculates your portfolio's total value and provides insights into daily changes, helping you stay informed without overwhelming complexity. If you're new to cryptocurrency, these platforms' straightforward interfaces are easy to navigate and provide helpful information like historical data and market trends.

If you manage a more extensive or more diverse portfolio, you may benefit from a dedicated portfolio-tracking app like Delta or Blockfolio (now FTX). These tools offer advanced features, including exchange integrations that sync your account data directly with the app. This means your portfolio updates automatically whenever you make a trade, saving time and reducing errors. These apps often include price alerts, news feeds, and in-depth analytics, making them ideal for investors looking for more comprehensive tracking.

For those who value full customization, creating a spreadsheet in Excel or Google Sheets can provide unmatched flexibility. While this requires more manual input, you can design the tracker to meet your needs, incorporating custom metrics and personalized performance summaries. Automated functions, like importing real-time price data using scripts, can add efficiency to this approach.

Whatever tool you choose, the key is finding a solution matching your expertise and trading style. A sound tracking system will allow you to focus on your strategy without losing sight of your overall portfolio performance.

Setting Up Alerts for Price Changes
Crypto prices can change dramatically in minutes, making constantly monitoring the market impractical. Alerts help you stay on top of key price movements, allowing you to act swiftly when needed.

Most portfolio-tracking apps and exchanges include built-in features for creating price alerts. These notifications can be customized to align with your goals, whether waiting to buy during a price dip or planning to sell at a specific target. For example, setting an alert to notify you when Bitcoin hits a certain threshold ensures you're prepared to make decisions without watching the market continuously.

Setting up price alerts is straightforward if you're using an app like Delta or Blockfolio. Select the cryptocurrency you want to track, specify the target price, and enable notifications. You'll receive a push notification on your device when the price is reached. Many exchanges like Binance also allow you to set similar alerts directly within their trading platform.

For more advanced monitoring, consider setting alerts for additional metrics, such as trading volume or market capitalization changes. These indicators provide a broader view of market activity, helping you identify trends that may not be immediately apparent through price alone.

News alerts are another valuable tool, particularly in a market heavily influenced by sentiment and announcements. Apps like Blockfolio often feature integrated news feeds, ensuring you stay informed about events that could impact your investments, such as regulatory developments or major partnerships.

Alerts are a practical way to manage your investments proactively, especially if you're tracking multiple assets or don't have time to monitor the market constantly.

Understanding Market Fluctuations
Cryptocurrency markets are renowned for their volatility, which can feel daunting to new investors. However, understanding the factors that drive market fluctuations can help you approach these changes with a calm and informed mindset.

The first significant factor is market sentiment. In crypto, sentiment often shifts based on news events, tweets, and online discussions. Positive developments, such as a major corporation announcing cryptocurrency adoption, can create a surge in prices. Conversely, negative events, like regulatory crackdowns, can lead to sharp declines. Staying informed through reliable news sources is essential for understanding how sentiment might affect your investments.

Another critical factor is supply and demand dynamics. Bitcoin, for instance, has a fixed supply of 21 million coins, creating scarcity that drives demand. Other cryptocurrencies, like Ethereum, have mechanisms to issue new coins, which can influence their price over time. Understanding the tokenomics of a cryptocurrency—how its supply and demand are managed—can give you valuable insights into its long-term potential.

Market cycles are also significant. Like traditional markets, cryptocurrency moves through accumulation, uptrend, distribution, and downtrend phases. For example, some investors may sell after rising prices to secure profits, leading to a pullback or correction. Recognizing these cycles can help you avoid buying at a peak or selling during a temporary dip.

External factors, such as macroeconomic conditions, also play a role. Events like inflation, changes in interest rates, or geopolitical tensions can influence crypto prices as investors shift between traditional assets and digital currencies. For example, Bitcoin is sometimes seen as a hedge against inflation, attracting demand during periods of economic uncertainty.

Lastly, whale activity—transactions by individuals or entities holding large amounts of cryptocurrency—can cause sudden price swings. Monitoring whale movements through blockchain explorers or specialized analytics tools can provide early warnings of potential market changes.

Understanding these dynamics equips you to navigate volatility more effectively. Instead of reacting emotionally to price fluctuations, you can interpret them as part of the broader market trends and adjust your strategy accordingly.

Developing a Consistent Tracking Routine

Consistency is key to managing your crypto investments successfully. Establishing a routine for tracking your portfolio ensures you stay informed without feeling overwhelmed by constant market noise.

Start by setting aside specific times to review your investments. Daily or weekly check-ins are often sufficient for long-term investors, while active traders may need to monitor their portfolios more frequently. Use this time to assess your portfolio's performance, check for news updates, and evaluate whether any adjustments are necessary.

Keep a record of your trades, including the reasons behind each decision. Over time, this practice can help you identify patterns in your behavior, such as buying impulsively during market hype. Reviewing your history enables you to refine your strategy and avoid repeating mistakes.

If you use multiple platforms or wallets, consolidate your tracking efforts into a single tool or spreadsheet. This provides a more straightforward overview of your investments and reduces the risk of overlooking assets.

Finally, remain flexible. The cryptocurrency market is constantly evolving, and your tracking methods should adapt as your portfolio grows or your goals change. Regularly evaluate whether your tools and strategies are still effective, and feel free to explore new apps or approaches if they better suit your needs.

Tracking cryptocurrency investments requires reliable tools, strategic alerts, and understanding market behavior. By choosing the right portfolio tracker, setting meaningful alerts, and interpreting market fluctuations wisely, you can confidently navigate the crypto space's volatility. As you develop a consistent tracking routine and refine your approach, you'll be better equipped to make informed decisions and achieve your financial goals. In the next chapter, we'll delve into advanced strategies for managing risk and maximizing returns, building on your established foundation in tracking your investments effectively.

CHAPTER 6: MANAGING RISKS IN CRYPTO INVESTING

Navigating the volatile cryptocurrency market can feel like riding a rollercoaster. While the potential for high returns attracts many investors, the risks are equally significant. Prices can swing wildly due to market sentiment, regulatory news, or technical issues, making it crucial to adopt a thoughtful and informed approach to manage these risks effectively. This chapter explores strategies to help you mitigate risks while participating in this dynamic market.

Understanding Cryptocurrency Volatility

Volatility is inherent to cryptocurrency markets. Unlike traditional investments, such as stocks or bonds, digital assets are influenced by unique factors that can amplify price swings. Recognizing these factors and their interplay is the first step to managing risk.

One of the primary drivers of volatility is **speculation**. The relatively nascent nature of cryptocurrency markets means that prices are often driven by future expectations rather than intrinsic value. News about potential regulatory changes, partnerships, or technological advancements can send prices soaring—or plummeting. For example, the announcement of a major corporation accepting Bitcoin as payment often creates a temporary spike in demand, while regulatory crackdowns can cause sell-offs.

Another significant factor is **low market capitalization**. While the market has grown substantially, it remains small compared to traditional financial markets. This makes cryptocurrencies more susceptible to large price swings caused by individual transactions, especially for smaller altcoins. For instance, a "whale" selling a large position can create temporary imbalances, triggering broader market reactions.

Moreover, a centralized authority to stabilize markets is needed to avoid unpredictability. Traditional stock markets have mechanisms like trading halts to curb extreme volatility, but cryptocurrency markets operate 24/7 without such safeguards.

Understanding these dynamics can help contextualize price movements and avoid emotional decision-making during market turbulence.

Risk Management Techniques
Successfully navigating the cryptocurrency market requires a disciplined approach to managing risk. Here are some practical strategies to protect your investments and reduce the impact of volatility.

Diversification
Diversification is a fundamental principle in any investment strategy. By spreading your funds across different cryptocurrencies, you reduce the risk of a single asset's poor performance affecting your overall portfolio.

Begin with **established cryptocurrencies** like Bitcoin and Ethereum, which tend to be more stable due to their market dominance and widespread adoption. From there, consider adding a mix of altcoins with varying levels of risk and utility. For instance, you might include stablecoins like USDC or USDT to provide a buffer against market volatility. Stablecoins are pegged to fiat currencies, offering a relatively stable store of value.

Diversification can also extend beyond cryptocurrencies. Allocating a portion of your portfolio to traditional investments like stocks, bonds, or real estate can provide additional stability.

Dollar-cost averaging (DCA)

Dollar-cost averaging is a strategy where you invest a fixed amount of money at regular intervals, regardless of the asset's price. This approach reduces the emotional impact of market swings, eliminating the pressure to time the market.

For example, instead of investing $1,000 in Bitcoin all at once, you invest $100 weekly over ten weeks. This strategy ensures that you buy more when prices are low and less when prices are high, averaging your purchase price over time.

DCA is particularly effective in volatile markets, mitigating the risk of making large investments during a price peak.

Setting Stop-Loss and Take-Profit Levels

Stop-loss and take-profit orders help automate your trading decisions, reducing the risk of emotional reactions to price changes.

> A **stop-loss order** automatically sells your asset when it reaches a specific price, limiting potential losses. For instance, if you buy Bitcoin at $30,000 and set a stop-loss at $28,000, your position will automatically close if the price drops to that level.
>
> A **take-profit order** locks in gains by selling when an asset reaches a specific price. For example, suppose Bitcoin rises to $35,000, and you've set a take-profit order at that level. In that case, your position will close, securing your profit.

These tools are particularly useful for active traders but can benefit long-term investors during extreme volatility.

Invest Only What You Can Afford to Lose

Cryptocurrency investing carries inherent risks, so investing only what you can afford to lose is crucial. Avoid using funds earmarked for essential expenses like rent, utilities, or emergency savings. Keeping your investments within a reasonable portion of your overall financial portfolio helps protect you from significant financial stress.

A good rule of thumb is to allocate no more than 5–10% of your total investment portfolio to cryptocurrencies, particularly if you're a beginner.

Maintain a Long-Term Perspective

While focusing on short-term gains is tempting, adopting a long-term perspective can help weather the market's ups and downs. Historical data shows that despite its volatility, Bitcoin has experienced significant growth. Rather than reacting impulsively, holding onto your investments through market fluctuations can yield better results. That said, it's important to periodically reassess your portfolio and ensure your holdings align with your financial goals and risk tolerance.

Dealing with Emotional Investing

Emotions are significant in investment decisions, particularly in volatile markets like cryptocurrency. Fear of missing out (FOMO) and panic selling are common pitfalls that can lead to poor decision-making.

Recognizing FOMO

FOMO often arises when an asset's price rapidly increases, and investors worry about missing out on potential gains. This can lead to impulsive buying at inflated prices and regret when the market corrects.

To combat FOMO, establish a clear investment strategy and stick to it. Avoid making decisions based on hype or short-term trends, and focus on the long-term potential of your investments.

Overcoming Panic Selling

Panic selling occurs when prices drop sharply, and investors sell their holdings for fear of further losses. While feeling anxious during a market downturn is natural, selling at the bottom locks in your losses and prevents you from benefiting from potential recoveries.

A predefined risk management plan, including stop-loss orders and a clear understanding of your investment horizon, can help you stay calm and avoid rash decisions during market dips.

Staying Informed Without Overloading

While staying informed is important, constantly monitoring prices or consuming excessive market news can increase anxiety and lead to emotional reactions. Set specific times to check your portfolio and focus on trusted sources of information rather than social media speculation.

Learning from Past Market Crashes

Historical market crashes in cryptocurrency offer invaluable lessons about risk management, the importance of diversification, and the need for a disciplined approach to investing. These events highlight the unique challenges of this volatile market and underscore opportunities for growth and the importance of learning from mistakes. We can identify patterns, understand common pitfalls, and develop strategies to safeguard our portfolios during turbulent times by analyzing past crashes.

The 2018 Bitcoin Bubble and Crypto Crash

In late 2017, Bitcoin experienced an extraordinary rise, surging from around $1,000 at the beginning of the year to nearly $20,000 by December. This meteoric ascent was largely driven by speculative mania, with retail investors entering the market in droves, many of whom had limited knowledge of cryptocurrency. Media hype and the fear of missing out (FOMO) fueled the rally, leading to unsustainable price levels.

However, the bubble burst in early 2018, triggering a prolonged bear market. Bitcoin's value plummeted, eventually stabilizing around $3,000 by the end of the year. The broader crypto market also suffered, with many altcoins losing 90% or more of their value.

Lessons Learned:
    Avoid Buying During Hype Cycles: Investors who purchased Bitcoin near its peak faced substantial losses. This underscores the importance of avoiding investments driven solely by hype and entering the market with a clear strategy.
    Understand Market Cycles: Like traditional financial markets, crypto operates in cycles. Recognizing the signs of a speculative bubble—such as unsustainable price growth and excessive media attention—can help you avoid buying at inflated prices.
    Invest for the Long Term: Despite the crash, Bitcoin eventually recovered, reaching new all-time highs in subsequent years. Long-term investors who held their assets through the downturn were rewarded, highlighting the benefits of a patient, long-term approach.

The 2022 Terra-LUNA Collapse
One of the most dramatic crypto crashes occurred in May 2022 with the collapse of Terra's ecosystem, including its algorithmic stablecoin UST and its sister token, LUNA. Terra's UST was designed to maintain a 1:1 peg to the US dollar through an intricate mechanism involving LUNA. However, this mechanism needed to be better understood and relied heavily on market confidence.

A cascading effect ensued when UST lost its peg: investors rapidly sold off UST, causing a sharp decline in LUNA's value and destabilizing it further. Within days, LUNA's price dropped by over 99%, erasing billions of dollars in value and devastating countless investors.

Lessons Learned:
    Beware of Over-Reliance on Unproven Technology: Terra's collapse highlighted the risks of investing

in experimental financial mechanisms. Algorithmic stablecoins, while innovative, lacked the robustness of traditional asset-backed stablecoins, making them vulnerable to systemic failure.

Diversification is Crucial: Many investors had concentrated their portfolios in LUNA, attracted by its high yields and rapid price growth. When the ecosystem collapsed, they faced catastrophic losses. Diversification across multiple assets and sectors could have mitigated the impact.

Do Your Due Diligence: Understanding the technology and risks behind a project is essential. Blindly chasing high returns without comprehending the underlying mechanics can lead to significant losses.

The Mt. Gox Hack (2014)

Before Bitcoin became a household name, the Mt. Gox exchange handled most transactions worldwide. In early 2014, Mt. Gox suffered a massive hack, losing 850,000 Bitcoins (worth approximately $450 million). The exchange declared bankruptcy, and many users lost their entire holdings.

The hack caused a sharp drop in Bitcoin's price, with the cryptocurrency losing nearly 50% of its value in the weeks following the news. This event eroded confidence in the nascent crypto market and highlighted the importance of security.

Lessons Learned:

Store Crypto in Personal Wallets: Leaving funds on an exchange exposes them to potential hacks or mismanagement. Hardware wallets and other forms of cold storage provide greater security by keeping your private keys offline.

Choose Reputable Platforms: Conduct thorough research before using an exchange. Look for platforms with strong security measures, regulatory compliance, and a proven track record.

Plan for the Worst-Case Scenario: Mt. Gox's collapse was a stark reminder of the importance of not keeping all your funds in one place. Splitting your holdings across multiple wallets and platforms can reduce the risk of total loss.

The COVID-19 Market Crash (March 2020)

The onset of the COVID-19 pandemic in early 2020 triggered a global financial crisis, and the cryptocurrency market was no exception. In March 2020, known as "Black Thursday," Bitcoin's price plummeted by nearly 50% daily, falling from around $8,000 to $4,000. Other cryptocurrencies experienced similar declines as panic selling gripped the market.

Despite the dramatic drop, the market rebounded quickly, with Bitcoin reaching new all-time highs by the end of the year. The rapid recovery highlighted crypto's resilience and growing appeal as an alternative asset class during economic uncertainty.

Lessons Learned:

Prepare for Sudden Downturns: The sharp decline in March 2020 was a reminder of crypto's volatility. A risk management plan, such as stop-loss orders or an emergency cash reserve, can help protect your portfolio during unexpected market shocks.

Seize Opportunities During Dips: While the crash devastated many, it also allowed long-term investors to accumulate assets at discounted prices. Those who bought during the dip reaped significant rewards as prices recovered.

Understand Correlations with Broader Markets: The crash demonstrated that cryptocurrency is not entirely insulated from traditional financial markets. Global events like the COVID-19 pandemic can impact traditional and digital assets.

The 2021 China Ban on Crypto

In 2021, China announced a sweeping ban on cryptocurrency mining and trading, citing concerns about energy consumption and financial stability. This news caused Bitcoin's price to drop from over $50,000 to around $30,000 within weeks. The ban forced miners to relocate, leading to a temporary decline in the Bitcoin network's hash rate.

Despite the initial panic, the market eventually recovered as mining operations moved to more crypto-friendly countries, and investor confidence returned.

Lessons Learned:
>**Regulatory Risks Are Real:** Governments significantly influence cryptocurrency markets, and regulatory changes can create volatility. Diversifying geographically by holding assets or engaging with exchanges in different jurisdictions can mitigate regulatory risks.
>**Crypto's Resilience:** The market's recovery following the China ban demonstrated its ability to adapt and thrive despite adverse conditions. This resilience reinforces the importance of maintaining a long-term perspective during periods of uncertainty.

How to Apply These Lessons
>**Diversification is Non-Negotiable:** Holding a mix of cryptocurrencies and other asset classes reduces the impact of a single asset's poor performance.
>**Do Your Research:** Understanding the fundamentals of your investment projects can help you avoid speculative bubbles and risky ventures.
>**Keep Security Front and Center:** Use personal wallets for storage, enable two-factor authentication, and avoid leaving large sums on exchanges.
>**Stay Calm During Crashes:** Panic selling locks in losses. By

maintaining a long-term perspective and focusing on your investment strategy, you can avoid knee-jerk reactions to market downturns.

Take Advantage of Opportunities: Market crashes often create buying opportunities for long-term investors. If you've researched and believe in an asset's fundamentals, a downturn can be an ideal time to accumulate.

Learning from past market crashes enables you to approach cryptocurrency investing with greater confidence and resilience. While no strategy can eliminate all risks, understanding the causes and consequences of volatility prepares you to navigate this dynamic market more effectively. As you continue to grow your portfolio, remember that patience, discipline, and education are your greatest allies in the ever-evolving world of cryptocurrency.

Developing a Risk Management Strategy

Investing in cryptocurrency offers substantial opportunities but comes with significant risks. To navigate the market effectively, it is essential to create a comprehensive risk management strategy. This involves setting clear investment goals, diversifying your portfolio, and applying effective tools like stop-loss and take-profit strategies. Implementing these strategies can mitigate risks and maximize returns while controlling your investments.

Setting Investment Goals

The foundation of any sound investment strategy is clarity about your goals. Knowing exactly what you want to achieve provides a roadmap for your decisions, keeps you focused, and prevents emotional reactions during volatile times. Start by understanding your purpose. Ask yourself why you're investing in cryptocurrency. Are you aiming to grow wealth over the long term, seeking short-term gains, or adding diversity to your broader investment portfolio? For example, suppose your goal is long-term wealth creation. In that case, you might focus on established cryptocurrencies like Bitcoin or Ethereum, known for their resilience and slower, steadier growth. Conversely, smaller altcoins with greater volatility could be more appealing if you target short-term profits.

Time horizons also play a pivotal role. Suppose you're investing with a 10-year outlook. In that case, you're more likely to endure short-term price swings without panic, knowing that your strategy is focused on overall growth. On the other hand, short-term investors need to be more vigilant, monitoring market trends closely to seize quick opportunities or mitigate losses.

Equally important is understanding your personal risk tolerance. How much financial loss can you absorb without stress? Some investors thrive on high-risk, high-reward scenarios, while others prefer stability. For instance, someone with a lower tolerance for risk might allocate only a small portion of their portfolio to crypto and stick to major coins. In contrast, a higher-risk investor might explore smaller, emerging projects.

Setting measurable targets provides clarity and structure. Instead of vague aspirations like "make a lot of money," define specific goals. You may aim for a 20% return within a year or grow your portfolio to $50,000 over five years. These targets serve as benchmarks to measure your progress and maintain discipline.

Finally, having an exit plan ensures you're prepared for any scenario. Decide when you'll sell—whether to take profits after achieving your target or minimize losses if prices drop below a certain level. For instance, you might sell half your holdings if they double in value, securing profits while leaving room for further growth. Exit plans remove the guesswork during critical moments, allowing you to make clear-headed decisions aligned with your goals.

Diversifying Your Digital Portfolio

Diversification is one of the most effective ways to manage risk, particularly in the volatile world of cryptocurrency. Spreading your investments across a range of assets reduces the impact of poor performance from any single asset on your overall portfolio.

Consider starting with large-cap cryptocurrencies like Bitcoin and Ethereum when constructing a diversified crypto portfolio. These coins are often considered safer bets due to their established networks, high liquidity, and widespread adoption. Bitcoin's role as a store of value, akin to digital gold, makes it a staple for many investors. On the other hand, Ethereum supports an extensive ecosystem of decentralized applications, offering growth potential and stability.

Beyond large caps, consider including altcoins to add variety and potential for higher returns. Altcoins like Solana or Polkadot offer unique advantages like faster transaction speeds or enhanced scalability. These coins come with increased risk but can also deliver outsized gains if they succeed. Balancing established assets with emerging projects creates stability and growth opportunities.

Including stablecoins like Tether (USDT) or USD Coin (USDC) provides a hedge against volatility. Stablecoins maintain value by pegging to fiat currencies, offering a safe haven during market downturns. They're also useful for liquidity, allowing you to quickly move funds between assets without relying on traditional banking systems.

Diversification isn't limited to coin types—it also involves spreading investments across different blockchain ecosystems. For instance, investing in Ethereum, Binance Smart Chain, and Polkadot reduces the risk tied to any single network's technical issues or regulatory hurdles. By participating in multiple ecosystems, you also benefit from innovations in different sectors.

Emerging fields like decentralized finance (DeFi) and non-fungible tokens (NFTs) offer further diversification. Platforms like Aave or Uniswap provide exposure to DeFi, enabling decentralized lending or trading opportunities. Meanwhile, NFTs tap into the world of digital collectibles and art, representing a unique and rapidly growing market.

That said, avoid over-diversifying. Holding too many assets can dilute your returns and make your portfolio cumbersome. A focused selection of 5–10 cryptocurrencies allows you to achieve diversity while maintaining control. Regularly rebalancing your portfolio ensures that it remains aligned with your original allocation. For instance, if Ethereum outperforms and becomes a disproportionately large part of your holdings, selling some ETH to reinvest in underperforming assets restores balance.

By diversifying wisely, you can protect your portfolio from sharp losses while positioning yourself for gains across various sectors and asset types.

Applying Stop-Loss and Take-Profit Strategies
Stop-loss and take-profit orders are invaluable tools for managing risk and ensuring disciplined decision-making. These predefined orders automate your trading process, helping avoid emotional reactions during volatile times.

A stop-loss order minimizes potential losses by selling an asset if its price falls to a specified level. For example, if you purchase Ethereum at $2,000, you might set a stop-loss at $1,800. If the price drops to $1,800, the order executes automatically, limiting your loss to 10%. Stop-loss orders are particularly useful in a market like cryptocurrency, where prices can drop dramatically quickly.

For longer-term investors, stop-loss levels might be lower, allowing for greater fluctuation without triggering a sale. For instance, you might set a stop-loss at 30% below your purchase price if you're confident in the asset's long-term potential. Conversely, short-term traders may use tighter limits, such as 5–10%, to protect capital during day-to-day price swings.

A trailing stop-loss order adds flexibility by adjusting the stop price as the asset's value rises. For instance, if Bitcoin increases from $20,000 to $25,000, a trailing stop-loss set at 10% would move to $22,500. This approach locks in profits while allowing for further upside.

Take-profit orders complement stop-losses by securing gains when an asset reaches a predetermined target price. If you buy Cardano (ADA) at $1.50 and set a take-profit at $2.00, the order will execute once ADA hits $2.00, ensuring you lock in a 33% gain. These orders help you resist the temptation to hold out for even higher prices, which could lead to losses if the market reverses.

Combining stop-loss and take-profit orders creates a defined range for your trades, protecting against significant losses while ensuring you capitalize on upward movements. For instance, if you buy Solana (SOL) at $50, you might set a stop-loss at $45 and a take-profit at $70. This strategy limits your downside risk to 10% while allowing for a 40% gain.

These strategies also remove the need for constant market monitoring, giving you peace of mind while protecting your investments. You can focus on broader market trends and long-term planning by automating critical decisions.

Managing risk in cryptocurrency investing requires a proactive and disciplined approach. Setting clear investment goals provides direction and helps you focus during turbulent times. Diversifying your portfolio across asset types, ecosystems, and sectors reduces exposure to individual risks. At the same time, stop-loss and take-profit orders offer structured and emotion-free decision-making. With a robust risk management strategy, you can confidently navigate the challenges of the crypto market and work toward achieving your financial goals.

Staying Informed and Avoiding Scams

While exciting and full of opportunities, the cryptocurrency landscape is also fraught with risks. Its decentralized nature, rapid technological evolution, and lack of regulatory oversight make it an attractive playground for fraudsters and scammers. Staying informed about potential risks and adopting rigorous security measures are critical to protect your investments and navigate the space safely. This chapter delves into recognizing scams, verifying trustworthy sources, and implementing best practices for secure transactions to help you safeguard your crypto journey.

Recognizing Common Scams and Fraud Tactics

Scams in the crypto space often prey on investor enthusiasm, greed, or lack of technical knowledge. Familiarizing yourself with these fraudulent tactics can save you from costly mistakes. One of the most persistent scams is the Ponzi scheme. These operations promise investors consistent and unrealistic returns, often cloaking their fraudulent nature behind complex jargon or supposedly advanced technology. The infamous BitConnect scam is a prime example. It lured investors with promises of guaranteed returns through a non-existent "trading bot." When the bubble burst, billions of dollars in investor funds evaporated, leaving countless victims in financial ruin.

Another scam that has plagued the crypto world is the rise of fake initial coin offerings (ICOs). These schemes often involve elaborate whitepapers, professional-looking websites, and exaggerated promises of revolutionary technologies. The 2017 ICO boom saw numerous such projects, many disappearing once funds were raised. Warning signs include:

    Anonymous teams.

    Lack of a working product.

Excessive focus on fundraising without clear objectives or a roadmap.

Phishing scams are another common threat. Fraudsters create fake websites or send deceptive emails that mimic trusted platforms to steal sensitive information like private keys or login credentials. For instance, a seemingly legitimate email from a crypto exchange might direct you to a replica website designed to capture your account details. Verifying URLs, avoiding links in unsolicited messages, and bookmarking official websites effectively counteract phishing attempts.

The allure of quick profits also drives pump-and-dump schemes. Coordinated groups artificially inflate the price of a low-value coin through aggressive promotion, only to sell their holdings at the peak, causing the price to crash. The victims, often retail investors who bought in at inflated prices, suffer substantial losses. Staying wary of unexplained surges in price and researching the coin's fundamentals can help you avoid falling into such traps.

Social media platforms and apps are also rife with fake giveaways and impersonation scams. Scammers posing as celebrities or influencers promise massive returns if you send them cryptocurrency, only to disappear with your funds. A good rule of thumb is to remember that legitimate projects or individuals will never ask you to send crypto to receive more in return.

Fake wallets and apps are another dangerous avenue for scams. These fraudulent applications claim to store your cryptocurrency securely but are designed to steal your funds. Only download wallets from reputable sources and verify their authenticity through community reviews and official channels.

By understanding these tactics, you can recognize the red flags and protect yourself from losing your investments to scams.

Always exercise caution, especially with offers that seem too good to be true.

Verifying Sources and Influencers

With cryptocurrency information often disseminated through social media, forums, and online influencers, distinguishing credible advice from biased or misleading opinions is vital. The sheer volume of information can be overwhelming. Still, a systematic approach to vetting sources can help you make informed decisions.

Begin by assessing the credibility of an influencer or source. Consider their background, expertise, and track record in the crypto space. Influencers with experience in finance, technology, or blockchain are more likely to offer reliable insights than anonymous accounts or self-proclaimed experts. LinkedIn profiles, prior publications, and affiliations with reputable organizations can lend credibility to their advice.

Objectivity is another key factor. Reliable sources provide balanced perspectives, highlighting an investment's opportunities and risks. Beware of influencers who exclusively promote specific projects without addressing potential downsides, as they may have financial incentives to do so. Transparency is a hallmark of trustworthiness; reputable influencers will disclose any partnerships or investments that may influence their opinions.

Cross-referencing information across multiple reputable sources is essential. For example, if you hear about a new project or token, check its website, official social media channels, and discussions on established platforms like CoinDesk, Decrypt, or Messari. Avoid relying solely on social media or forums, which can often amplify misinformation or hype.

Online communities like Reddit or Telegram can be valuable for learning and discussing crypto topics but should not replace in-depth research. Anonymous posts and crowd sentiment can lead to herd behavior, where decisions are driven more by emotion than analysis. Use these platforms to gather diverse viewpoints but validate claims with independent research.

Verifying your sources minimizes the risk of acting on biased or false information, empowering you to make data-driven investment decisions.

Best Practices for Secure Transactions
Securing your cryptocurrency transactions is as critical as choosing the right investments. Blockchain technology's decentralized and irreversible nature means that mistakes or breaches can permanently lose funds. Adopting robust security practices helps safeguard your assets and ensures peace of mind.

A fundamental step is enabling two-factor authentication (2FA) on all crypto accounts. Authenticator apps like Google Authenticator or Authy provide a layer of security beyond passwords, reducing the likelihood of unauthorized access. While SMS-based 2FA is an option, it could be more secure due to the risk of SIM-swapping attacks. For higher security, use app-based authentication wherever possible.

Protecting your private keys and recovery phrases is paramount. These are the keys to your wallet, and losing them means losing access to your funds. Store them offline, such as on paper, in a secure safe or lockbox. Never store this information digitally, as hackers can target it.

For significant holdings, consider using a hardware wallet like Ledger or Trezor. These devices store your crypto offline, making them immune to online attacks. They are particularly suitable for long-term investors who prioritize security over convenience.

When sending cryptocurrency, double-check the recipient's wallet address to ensure accuracy. Malware can alter copied addresses in your clipboard, redirecting funds to a scammer.

Conducting a small test transaction before transferring large sums is a prudent step to confirm the address and avoid costly errors.

Public Wi-Fi networks pose additional risks and are vulnerable to man-in-the-middle attacks. If you must access your wallet or exchange on public Wi-Fi, use a Virtual Private Network (VPN) to encrypt your connection and protect your data.

Limit the amount of cryptocurrency you store on exchanges. While exchanges are convenient for trading, they are also prime targets for hackers. Move your assets to a private wallet for enhanced security, and only keep the necessary amount in exchange for active trades.

Staying informed about the latest security developments is another essential practice. Follow updates from your wallet provider or exchange, as they often release patches and recommendations to address emerging threats. Awareness of new vulnerabilities or scams can help you proactively secure your assets.

By implementing these practices, you can protect your investments from scams, theft, and human error. The effort you put into securing your transactions pays off in the long run, giving you confidence in navigating the dynamic crypto landscape.

The Path Forward: Informed and Secure Investing
The cryptocurrency market offers immense potential but requires vigilance to navigate safely. Recognizing common scams, verifying trustworthy sources, and securing your transactions form the cornerstone of a sound investment strategy. You protect your assets and peace of mind by staying informed and adopting rigorous security measures.

As you continue your journey, remember that the dynamic nature of cryptocurrency requires ongoing learning and adaptation. In the next chapter, we'll explore advanced tools and analytical strategies to help you evaluate crypto projects and make more informed investment decisions, empowering you to maximize your potential in this exciting new frontier.

CHAPTER 7: UNDERSTANDING CRYPTO TAXES AND REGULATIONS

Investing in cryptocurrency offers vast potential but comes with unique challenges, including navigating the complexities of taxation and regulations. Cryptocurrencies are treated differently from traditional financial assets, with tax authorities viewing them as property rather than currency. This distinction creates a unique set of rules and responsibilities for investors. Failing to meet these obligations can result in significant penalties, so understanding how to manage crypto taxes is critical. This chapter delves into the fundamentals of crypto taxation, the importance of meticulous record-keeping, and the forms required to comply with regulations. Understanding these essentials allows you to avoid pitfalls and manage your crypto investments responsibly.

Basics of Crypto Taxation
Despite their decentralized nature, cryptocurrencies fall under the purview of tax authorities worldwide. In most jurisdictions, crypto transactions are taxed based on capital gains and losses, similar to how property or stocks are treated. Recognizing taxable events and their implications is essential for maintaining compliance.

One of the most common taxable events is buying and selling cryptocurrency. For instance, if you purchased Bitcoin at $20,000 and sold it at $30,000, the $10,000 profit is considered a capital gain. This gain is taxable, and the tax rate will depend on how long you hold the asset. Holding crypto for less than a year usually subjects the gain to short-term capital gains tax, which aligns with your ordinary income tax rate. Holding it for over a year typically qualifies for long-term capital gains tax, which is often lower. Similarly, if you sold Bitcoin at $15,000, resulting in a $5,000 loss, that loss could offset other capital gains, potentially reducing your overall tax burden.

Trading one cryptocurrency for another, such as swapping Bitcoin for Ethereum, is another taxable event. Even though you haven't converted to fiat currency, trading triggers a taxable gain or loss. For example, if you acquired Bitcoin at $20,000 and traded it for Ethereum when Bitcoin was valued at $25,000, you'd need to report a $5,000 gain. The value of the Ethereum you receive becomes your new cost basis for future tax calculations.

Using crypto to purchase goods or services also constitutes a taxable event. Whether buying a coffee or a car, the difference between the crypto's value and cost basis must be reported as a capital gain or loss. For instance, if you paid for a $50 dinner using Bitcoin acquired at $40, you'd report a $10 gain.

Earning crypto through mining, staking, or as payment for services introduces another layer of complexity. In these cases, the crypto is treated as ordinary income, and its fair market value at receipt determines the amount you must report. For example, if you mined Ethereum worth $2,000, you'd report $2,000 as income. If you later sell the mined Ethereum, any additional gains or losses would fall under capital gains tax.

Depending on your jurisdiction, shifting cryptocurrency may or may not trigger tax obligations. In many cases, gifting is not taxable for the giver. However, the recipient may face tax obligations if they sell the gifted crypto. Always check your local regulations to understand the implications of gifting assets.

Understanding these taxable events is crucial for compliance. No matter how small, every crypto-related transaction carries potential tax implications, so staying informed is key to avoiding unexpected liabilities.

Record-Keeping Essentials

Thorough record-keeping is the cornerstone of effective crypto tax management. Cryptocurrencies' decentralized and anonymous nature requires investors to take personal responsibility for tracking transactions. With the fast-paced nature of the crypto market, accurate and organized records are indispensable.

Start by recording all purchase and sale dates for your cryptocurrency transactions. The holding period of each asset—whether it's less than a year or more than a year—affects the tax rate applied to any gains. For instance, holding Ethereum for 14 months before selling qualifies you for long-term capital gains tax, often lower than the short-term rate applied to assets held for only 10 months.

Documenting purchase and sale prices is equally important. Your cost basis—the original value of your crypto at purchase—is the foundation for calculating capital gains or losses. For example, if you bought 1 Bitcoin at $30,000 and sold it at $40,000, the $10,000 gain must be reported. This calculation becomes more complex with crypto-to-crypto trades, where the fair market value of both assets must be recorded at the time of the transaction.

Income-related transactions, such as mining or staking rewards, require special attention. Record the fair market value of the crypto at the time you received it, as this determines the income you must report. If you later sell or trade these rewards, additional gains or losses must be calculated based on the new cost basis.

Keeping track of wallet addresses is another crucial step, with multiple wallets and exchanges often in play, and organizing which transactions are associated with which wallets can streamline your record-keeping process. For example, suppose you hold assets in a cold storage wallet and a centralized exchange. In that case, maintaining separate logs for each ensures transparency and accuracy.

Crypto tax software like CoinTracker, Koinly, or CryptoTrader.Tax can simplify this process. These tools allow you to import data directly from exchanges and wallets, automatically calculating gains, losses, and income. They also generate tax reports in formats compatible with local regulations, saving time and reducing the likelihood of errors.

Finally, retain all records for the duration required by your tax authority. In the US, for example, the IRS recommends keeping records for at least three years or longer in certain circumstances. Physical and digital backups of transaction logs, receipts, and tax forms provide added security in case of an audit.

Tax Forms and Reporting
Filing taxes for cryptocurrency investments requires familiarity with specific forms and reporting requirements. Several vital documents are essential for compliance in the US, but the general principles apply to many jurisdictions.

Form 8949 is the starting point for reporting capital gains and losses. Each taxable event must be listed, including the dates of acquisition and sale, cost basis, proceeds, and resulting gain or loss. Transactions are divided into short-term and long-term categories, as the tax rates differ. For instance, selling Bitcoin held for six months would fall under short-term gains, while selling Ethereum held for 18 months would qualify as a long-term gain.

Schedule D summarizes the total capital gains and losses reported on Form 8949. This form calculates your net gain or loss for the year, which is then used to determine your tax liability. If your losses exceed your gains, you can deduct the excess, up to certain limits, to reduce your taxable income.

Income from mining, staking, or payment in crypto must be reported on Schedule 1 as additional income. If you're self-employed and receive crypto as payment, report this income on Schedule C, which accounts for business earnings and expenses. Self-employment taxes may also apply in this case.

Some exchanges issue Form 1099-K or Form 1099-B, summarizing your transactions for the year. To ensure accuracy, these forms are sent to you and the IRS, so it's essential to reconcile them with your records. Any discrepancies could trigger an audit.

If you hold assets on foreign exchanges exceeding certain thresholds, you may need to file an FBAR (Foreign Bank Account Report). This form is mandatory for US taxpayers with significant foreign accounts, including crypto holdings on non-U.S.-based platforms.

For those experiencing net losses, capital loss carryover provisions allow you to offset future gains, potentially lowering your tax burden in subsequent years. For example, if your 2023 crypto investments resulted in a $5,000 loss, and your 2024 investments yield a $3,000 gain, the remaining $2,000 loss can still be applied.

Given the complexity of crypto taxes, consulting a tax professional specializing in digital assets is highly recommended. Regulations and reporting requirements constantly evolve, and expert advice ensures compliance while optimizing your tax strategy.

Navigating the Complexities of Crypto Taxes
Taxation in cryptocurrency may seem daunting, but breaking it down into actionable steps—understanding taxable events, maintaining meticulous records, and filing the correct forms—

makes the process more manageable. With proper preparation, you can fulfill your obligations confidently and focus on maximizing the potential of your investments. As regulations continue to evolve, staying informed and proactive ensures you remain compliant while minimizing financial risks. In the next section, we'll explore the regulatory landscape, helping you understand the global framework shaping the future of cryptocurrency.

Regulations Around the World

Cryptocurrency regulations form a mosaic of global approaches, reflecting the balance governments seek between fostering innovation and ensuring financial security. While some countries adopt supportive frameworks to position themselves as leaders in digital finance, others impose strict rules or outright bans to address fraud, tax evasion, and financial stability concerns. For crypto investors, understanding the regulatory environment is as crucial as mastering market trends, as compliance with these rules impacts everything from trading to taxation. This chapter explores the regulatory landscape across key countries, emerging trends, and their implications for investors.

The Diverse Global Landscape of Crypto Regulation

The regulatory approaches of nations worldwide reflect their economic priorities, risk tolerances, and attitudes toward innovation. While some governments welcome cryptocurrencies as a driver of technological progress, others view them as a disruptive force requiring tight control. For investors, this diversity means that your experience with crypto can vary dramatically depending on where you live or trade.

In the United States, cryptocurrency is subject to a patchwork of rules overseen by multiple federal agencies. The Securities and Exchange Commission (SEC) has been particularly active in asserting authority over cryptocurrencies, which it considers securities, as seen in its actions against several Initial Coin

Offerings (ICOs) that failed to meet compliance standards. For US investors, this means understanding whether the crypto assets they trade fall under securities regulations. Tax obligations further complicate the picture, as the IRS classifies cryptocurrencies as property, requiring meticulous reporting of gains, losses, and taxable events. Adding to the complexity, exchanges must adhere to stringent Anti-Money Laundering (AML) and Know Your Customer (KYC) protocols, ensuring compliance but potentially deterring privacy-conscious users.

Across the Atlantic, the European Union (EU) has adopted a more standardized approach through its upcoming Markets in Crypto-Assets (MiCA) regulation. Designed to harmonize rules across member states, MiCA aims to provide legal clarity for crypto projects while enhancing consumer protections. Investors in the EU will benefit from uniform regulations but may face stricter compliance requirements. Individual nations within the bloc, such as Germany, stand out for specific policies like tax exemptions for crypto held longer than a year, a feature appealing to long-term investors.

Japan is often cited as a model of balanced regulation. By recognizing Bitcoin as a legal tender in 2017, Japan became a global hub for cryptocurrency activity. Its Financial Services Agency (FSA) requires exchanges to register, ensuring robust consumer protections. At the same time, taxation policies on crypto gains encourage careful planning. Japan's proactive stance demonstrates how thoughtful regulation can foster a thriving crypto ecosystem while mitigating risks.

On the other hand, China has adopted one of the most restrictive approaches to cryptocurrency. A sweeping ban on trading and mining activities has effectively pushed much of the market underground or out of the country. Despite this, China's development of a Central Bank Digital Currency (CBDC), the digital yuan, highlights its interest in retaining control over digital financial innovations while sidelining decentralized alternatives.

In contrast, Singapore has emerged as a haven for crypto innovation. With no capital gains tax and a supportive regulatory framework under its Payment Services Act (PSA), the city-state attracts blockchain startups and institutional investors. However, the Monetary Authority of Singapore (MAS) enforces strict AML and KYC rules, balancing openness with safeguards.

The United Kingdom, while still navigating its post-Brexit regulatory identity, has implemented measures to control certain crypto activities. The Financial Conduct Authority (FCA) requires exchanges to register and comply with AML standards, and it has banned retail access to high-risk derivatives. For UK investors, these regulations mean fewer options but potentially greater protections.

These varying approaches underscore how national priorities shape crypto regulation. Investors must stay informed about local laws, as regulations directly affect trading, taxation, and investment strategies.

Emerging Trends in Cryptocurrency Regulation
As cryptocurrency matures, regulatory trends converge around common themes, reflecting global efforts to address opportunities and risks. These trends reveal how governments and regulators are preparing for the growing influence of digital assets.

One of the most prominent trends is the tightening of AML and KYC requirements. Governments are increasingly concerned about using cryptocurrencies for illicit activities, from money laundering to tax evasion. Exchanges and platforms now face heightened scrutiny, with many required to verify user identities and report suspicious transactions. While this creates a safer environment for legitimate investors, it raises concerns about data privacy and operational costs. Navigating exchanges with robust compliance policies has become a standard practice for investors.

Stablecoins, often viewed as a bridge between traditional finance and crypto, have also come under regulatory scrutiny. Their ability to maintain a stable value tied to fiat currencies makes them attractive for transactions and savings, but concerns about their reserves and systemic risks have prompted action. For instance, the US Treasury has proposed legislation to regulate stablecoins similarly to banks, requiring issuers to hold sufficient reserves. Investors relying on stablecoins for liquidity or DeFi activities should monitor these developments closely, as stricter oversight could alter the landscape.

Taxation is another evolving area. Tax authorities worldwide are improving their capacity to track cryptocurrency transactions, with some requiring exchanges to share customer data. This increased enforcement ensures compliance but adds complexity for investors, who must maintain detailed records to avoid penalties. In Australia, for instance, the tax office collaborates with exchanges to identify unreported gains. At the same time, India recently introduced a tax on crypto transactions, signaling a shift toward stricter oversight.

The rise of decentralized finance (DeFi) platforms poses unique challenges for regulators. These platforms operate without intermediaries and are difficult to regulate under traditional frameworks. As authorities explore how to apply AML and investor protection rules to DeFi, users should be aware that regulatory changes could impact platform access or functionality.

Finally, the emergence of CBDCs reflects a growing interest among central banks in digitizing national currencies. While CBDCs promise the benefits of cryptocurrency—such as faster transactions and reduced costs—they also allow governments to maintain control over monetary policy. For investors, the rollout of CBDCs could introduce competition with private cryptocurrencies, influencing demand and regulatory focus.

These trends illustrate the dynamic nature of cryptocurrency regulation. Investors attuned to these developments can better anticipate changes affecting their portfolios.

The Investor's Perspective: Navigating Regulatory Impacts
For cryptocurrency investors, regulations can feel like both a safety net and an obstacle. They provide structure and legitimacy to the market but also introduce complexities that can be challenging to navigate. Understanding how regulations affect key aspects of investing is essential for adapting to this environment.

Regulations often dictate the availability of trading platforms and services. For example, US investors may be restricted from using certain international exchanges lacking local compliance. While these limitations can reduce access to specific coins or features, they also ensure that regulated platforms offer greater security and consumer protections. Choosing compliant exchanges can safeguard investments against fraud and operational risks even with fewer options.

Compliance requirements, particularly around taxes, are another significant factor. Investors must report every taxable event, from trading to earning staking rewards. This obligation demands meticulous record-keeping, which can be time-consuming without the right tools. However, staying compliant avoids penalties and builds confidence in the legitimacy of crypto investing. Utilizing software like Koinly or seeking professional advice can streamline this process, making it manageable even for active traders.

Privacy concerns also play a role in shaping investor behavior. While stricter AML and KYC rules enhance security, they reduce the anonymity traditionally associated with cryptocurrency. For privacy-conscious investors, decentralized exchanges or privacy-focused coins like Monero may offer alternatives, though these come with their own risks and regulatory uncertainties.

Regulations can also impact portfolio returns. For instance, leverage or derivatives trading restrictions may limit opportunities for high-risk, high-reward strategies. Conversely, enhanced oversight can reduce market volatility, benefiting long-term investors seeking stability. Recognizing these trade-offs allows investors to align their strategy with regulatory realities.

Finally, regulations influence market sentiment and adoption. Positive regulatory developments, such as approving a Bitcoin ETF in certain markets, can drive institutional interest and boost prices. Conversely, restrictive measures, like China's mining ban, can create short-term volatility. Understanding these dynamics helps investors navigate market shifts and capitalize on opportunities.

Adapting to a Regulated Crypto Future
The regulatory landscape for cryptocurrency is evolving rapidly, reflecting the growing importance of digital assets in the global economy. While navigating these changes may require additional effort, understanding the rules allows investors to protect their portfolios, comply with laws, and benefit from the increasing legitimacy of the market. You can adapt your strategies to thrive in this dynamic environment by staying informed about global and local regulations. The following section will explore practical tools and techniques for aligning your investments with tax and regulatory requirements, ensuring a secure and compliant approach to crypto investing.

Staying Compliant
Navigating the rapidly evolving cryptocurrency landscape requires more than just strategic investment decisions; it demands diligent compliance with tax and regulatory requirements. Governments worldwide are increasingly

scrutinizing crypto assets, and staying compliant is essential to avoid penalties, maintain peace of mind, and uphold the legitimacy of your investments. As regulations become stricter and reporting requirements more detailed, understanding the nuances of compliance becomes an indispensable part of crypto investing.

Simplifying Compliance with Crypto Tax Software
For many investors, managing the tax obligations associated with cryptocurrency can feel overwhelming. The decentralized nature of crypto and the variety of taxable events means that manual tracking can quickly become unmanageable. This is where crypto tax software proves invaluable.

These tools streamline the complex process of tracking transactions, calculating gains, and generating reports. Tax software can automate data collection by integrating directly with exchanges and wallets, ensuring that every transaction—whether a small purchase or a significant trade—is accounted for. API integration provides real-time updates, syncing transaction data directly from the platforms you use. For exchanges or wallets that don't support APIs, the ability to upload CSV files means you can still maintain accurate records without manual entry.

Beyond simplifying data organization, tax software categorizes transactions based on their nature. It automatically distinguishes between purchasing, selling, or trading cryptocurrencies, calculating capital gains and losses accordingly. For those earning crypto through staking, mining, or other forms of income, the software captures the fair market value of the assets at the time of receipt, ensuring accurate income tax reporting.

At the end of the fiscal year, tax software generates detailed reports tailored to the requirements of your jurisdiction. Whether it's Form 8949 for US investors or equivalents for other countries, these reports reduce the guesswork in filing taxes. Many platforms also offer tools for tax optimization, such as suggesting strategies to reduce taxable gains and making compliance manageable and efficient.

Avoiding Common Compliance Pitfalls
Despite the availability of tools and resources, many investors still make avoidable mistakes regarding crypto compliance. These errors often stem from misconceptions about tax laws or underestimating the importance of meticulous record-keeping. One of the most frequent oversights is the failure to report all transactions. Some investors mistakenly believe that only crypto sold for fiat is taxable.

However, crypto-to-crypto trades, mining rewards, and even staking income are taxable in most jurisdictions.

Another common pitfall is needing to track and report the fair market value of crypto earned through non-trading activities, such as mining or receiving airdrops. The fair market value of these assets at the time of receipt is critical for accurate income reporting, yet it needs to be noticed.

Errors in calculating cost basis can also lead to inaccuracies. The cost basis determines a crypto asset's original value for calculating capital gains or losses. For investors using multiple exchanges or wallets, tracking the cost basis across platforms can become complicated, increasing the likelihood of mistakes.

Failing to maintain adequate records is another significant issue. Responding to audits or inquiries from tax authorities can only become easier with detailed documentation. Transaction histories, wallet addresses, and records of exchange activity should be preserved for several years, as required by your jurisdiction.

By understanding these pitfalls and leveraging tools like tax software to automate processes, investors can minimize the risk of errors and ensure compliance with local tax laws.

Preparing for Future Regulatory Changes

The regulatory environment for cryptocurrency is dynamic, with governments and institutions continually adapting their approaches. As adoption grows, so does the need for investors to remain flexible and informed. Staying updated on regulatory news is vital, not just within your own country but globally. Policies implemented in major markets, such as the United States or the European Union, often set trends that other countries may follow.

Consider following reliable crypto news outlets and regulatory announcements to keep pace with these changes. Establishing relationships with crypto-savvy tax professionals can also provide an edge. These experts monitor regulation changes and help you adapt your strategy, whether by identifying new opportunities for tax savings or guiding you through updated reporting requirements.

One significant area of change is the increasing focus on international compliance. Many governments are implementing stricter requirements for reporting foreign accounts or assets. Understanding cross-border regulations will be essential if you hold crypto on an international exchange or in a foreign wallet.

Privacy regulations, too, are evolving. While AML and KYC measures enhance security, they also impact the anonymity that once characterized cryptocurrency. Future regulations could require platforms to implement stricter identity verification processes or impose limitations on privacy-focused coins. For investors, this means being prepared to provide documentation and understanding how new rules may affect their preferred platforms.

Tax policies are another area to watch. Governments may introduce specific taxes for digital assets, such as wealth or transaction taxes. These changes could influence strategies, such as the timing of asset sales or the decision to hold long-term.

You can navigate these changes effectively while maintaining compliance by staying proactive—organizing records, consulting professionals, and planning for regulatory shifts.

Practical Strategies for Staying Compliant
Remaining compliant requires more than awareness; it demands a commitment to proactive and organized practices. Reviewing your portfolio and transaction history ensures your records are complete and current. If you're using multiple wallets or exchanges, consolidating data into a single system, such as tax software, simplifies management. For those who earn income through crypto activities like mining or staking, setting aside some earnings for taxes can prevent surprises during tax season. Keeping a separate account or wallet for this purpose can make budgeting easier.

Investors should also be prepared for audits or inquiries. Keeping digital and physical copies of tax filings, transaction records, and supporting documentation ensures that you can respond quickly to any requests from tax authorities.

Finally, consider the benefits of consistent learning. The crypto landscape constantly evolves, and staying informed can give you a strategic advantage. Attend webinars, join crypto communities, or subscribe to educational platforms to stay ahead of the curve.

Compliance as a Cornerstone of Crypto Investing
Compliance is not just a legal obligation; it's a cornerstone of responsible investing. By understanding the nuances of crypto taxation, avoiding common mistakes, and preparing for future regulatory changes, you can protect your assets and ensure the longevity of your investment strategy. While navigating compliance may seem daunting, the tools and

resources available today make it easier than ever to meet your obligations. As the crypto industry matures, staying compliant will safeguard your investments and contribute to the broader acceptance and stability of digital assets.

CHAPTER 8: BUILDING A LONG-TERM CRYPTO STRATEGY

Developing a sustainable and effective long-term strategy for cryptocurrency investing requires thoughtful consideration of your personal goals, risk tolerance, and preferred level of involvement in the market. With its unique volatility and rapid evolution, the crypto market offers opportunities that can be maximized through tailored approaches. Whether you're drawn to active management or prefer a hands-off strategy, the foundation of successful investing lies in aligning your methods with your financial aspirations and emotional resilience.

Understanding Investment Styles: Day Trading vs. Long-Term Holding

Adopting a day trading or long-term holding approach is pivotal, as these styles differ significantly in execution, demands, and outcomes. Each has merits and challenges, but success hinges on choosing a strategy that fits your temperament and lifestyle.

Day trading thrives on the volatility of cryptocurrency markets. With prices capable of swinging dramatically within minutes or hours, day traders aim to capitalize on short-term fluctuations. This style requires close monitoring of the market, technical analysis skills, and the ability to make rapid decisions under pressure. While day trading can yield substantial profits, it demands discipline and mental resilience, as losses are as frequent as gains. Moreover, the frequent transactions associated with day trading can incur significant fees, which may erode profits over time.

Conversely, long-term holding, or HODLing, adopts a more straightforward philosophy: buy and hold. This approach is rooted in the belief that cryptocurrency markets will appreciate over the long term despite short-term volatility. By holding onto assets for extended periods, investors can avoid the stress of daily price fluctuations and reduce transaction costs. However, the simplicity of this strategy doesn't shield it from challenges. Long-term holders must possess the patience and confidence to weather market downturns, trusting in their chosen assets' underlying value and potential.

The choice between these strategies depends on your time availability, risk appetite, and level of market engagement. If you enjoy analyzing trends and are comfortable with high-risk, fast-paced environments, day trading might suit you. If you're seeking a more hands-off approach emphasizing long-term growth, HODLing offers stability amid the market's turbulence.

Active vs. Passive Investment Approaches
Beyond the choice of trading style, investors must also decide between active and passive investment approaches, each offering distinct advantages and challenges. Active investing requires regular involvement, allowing you to respond to market movements, identify opportunities, and optimize your portfolio in real-time. Passive investing, conversely, is centered on building a diversified portfolio and holding it with minimal interference, letting the market's natural growth determine returns.

Active investing appeals to those who thrive on engagement and enjoy tracking trends, analyzing news, and responding to shifts in sentiment. You can capitalize on emerging opportunities and dynamically mitigate risks by actively managing your portfolio. For example, an active investor might allocate funds to a promising new blockchain project, reallocate holdings based on performance, or exit a position during a market downturn.

However, the demands of active investing can be intense. It requires time, research, emotional control, and the willingness to absorb transaction costs associated with frequent trades.

Passive investing suits those who prefer a more relaxed approach. Instead of reacting to short-term volatility, passive investors focus on long-term trends, often employing strategies like dollar-cost averaging (DCA) to reduce the impact of market fluctuations. A passive investor might regularly invest a fixed amount in Bitcoin or Ethereum regardless of their current price, gradually building a position over time. While this approach minimizes stress and trading fees, it also means missing out on potential gains from rapid market movements.

Your choice between active and passive strategies should align with your lifestyle and investment goals. It is rewarding to have the time and expertise to manage your portfolio actively. If you're seeking simplicity and long-term stability, a passive approach may better serve your needs.

Matching Strategy to Goals: Finding the Right Fit
Finding the investment strategy that best aligns with your financial objectives involves introspection and a clear understanding of your circumstances. Consider your risk tolerance first. Cryptocurrency's inherent volatility means that even the most conservative strategies involve some risk. Evaluate how much uncertainty you will tolerate without losing confidence or succumbing to emotional decision-making.

For example, if you're comfortable with potential short-term losses for the promise of higher returns, active investing or day trading may align with your risk profile. However, if significant volatility is stressful, adopting a long-term holding or passive strategy could provide greater peace of mind.

Your time commitment is another crucial factor. Active strategies require continuous monitoring and engagement with the market, which may not be feasible for those with demanding jobs or other responsibilities. Passive strategies, by contrast, require only periodic adjustments, freeing you to focus on other priorities.

Finally, consider your long-term financial goals. Are you looking to generate short-term income or build wealth over decades? If your goal is to grow a retirement fund or support a child's education in 15 years, long-term holding combined with dollar-cost averaging might be the most practical approach. If you're looking for additional income to supplement your day job, active investing or a hybrid strategy could be more appropriate.

Balancing Approaches with a Hybrid Strategy

A hybrid strategy can combine the best aspects of active and passive investing, providing flexibility and balance. For instance, you might allocate 80% of your portfolio to established, long-term assets like Bitcoin and Ethereum while dedicating the remaining 20% to high-risk, high-reward trades in emerging altcoins or DeFi projects.

This approach allows you to participate in the excitement and potential gains of active trading while maintaining a stable foundation. A hybrid strategy enables you to experiment with different styles without overcommitting, making it a valuable learning tool for new investors.

Adapting and Evolving Over Time

Investment strategies are not static; they evolve as your experience grows and your financial circumstances change. A strategy that works for you today may need adjustment in the future. Reviewing your portfolio and reassessing your goals can ensure your approach aligns with your needs.

For example, an investor who begins with active trading might transition to a more passive strategy over time, focusing on long-term growth as their understanding of the market deepens. Conversely, long-term holders might allocate a portion of their portfolio to active trades if they identify compelling opportunities.

Adaptability is key in the ever-changing world of cryptocurrency. By remaining open to adjustments and continually educating yourself, you can build a resilient, long-term strategy that adapts to the market's evolution and personal growth.

Building a long-term crypto strategy is about finding the right balance between engagement and stability, risk and reward, and short-term goals versus long-term aspirations. Whether you trade actively, hold assets for the future, or adopt a hybrid approach, the most important factor is staying true to your goals and maintaining the discipline to see your strategy through. By tailoring your approach to your unique circumstances, you'll be well-positioned to navigate the complexities of cryptocurrency investing and achieve your financial objectives. In the next chapter, we'll discuss the importance of diversification and how to construct a balanced crypto portfolio to mitigate risks and maximize potential returns.

Analyzing Coins and Projects
Investing in cryptocurrency for the long term demands a clear understanding of the assets you choose to include in your portfolio. With thousands of coins and tokens vying for attention, identifying the ones with strong foundations and promising futures is a challenge that requires both diligence and strategic analysis. By focusing on key elements such as the fundamentals of a project, market trends, and technical indicators, you can build a resilient portfolio designed to weather the inherent volatility of the crypto market. This chapter will delve into fundamental and technical analysis and the tools to help you make informed decisions.

Understanding Fundamental Analysis
Fundamental analysis is the backbone of long-term investing. It

involves evaluating the intrinsic value of a cryptocurrency by examining its use case, development team, and overall market position. While speculative price spikes may attract attention, a project's foundational strength often determines its longevity.

The team behind a cryptocurrency project is often a reliable indicator of its potential. Experienced developers with a track record in blockchain technology or related fields lend credibility to the project. For example, Ethereum's initial success can be attributed, in part, to its co-founder, Vitalik Buterin, whose deep understanding of blockchain and decentralized applications set the foundation for its innovation. Projects that openly share their team members' expertise, engage transparently with the public, and cultivate partnerships with reputable organizations are generally more trustworthy.

Examining a project's use case is equally important. A cryptocurrency must solve a real-world problem or introduce a meaningful innovation to have long-term value. Bitcoin, for instance, was designed as a decentralized alternative to traditional fiat currencies, while Ethereum's smart contract functionality opened the door for decentralized finance (DeFi) and non-fungible tokens (NFTs). Consider whether a project addresses a genuine need or if its token serves a critical purpose within its ecosystem. Tokens with clear utility—enabling transactions, governance, or staking—are more likely to sustain value.

The strength of a project's community is another vital component of fundamental analysis. Engaged communities often act as advocates, fostering adoption and resilience. A project with a dedicated base of developers and users is more likely to adapt to challenges and thrive over time. Platforms like Telegram, Twitter, and Reddit offer insights into the vibrancy of a project's community. Regular updates, transparent communication, and responsiveness to user feedback all indicate a project that prioritizes its supporters.

By thoroughly researching these aspects, you can distinguish projects with genuine potential from those that rely on hype. Cryptocurrencies with strong teams, practical use cases, and active communities are better positioned to navigate the evolving market landscape.

Exploring Technical Analysis

While fundamental analysis focuses on intrinsic value, technical analysis (TA) provides insights into market trends and price movements. By studying historical price data and patterns, you can make more informed decisions about when to enter or exit a position.

Charts are the foundation of technical analysis, visually representing an asset's price over time. Candlestick charts, for instance, reveal details about opening and closing prices, highs, and lows during specific time frames. Recognizing patterns like "head and shoulders" or "ascending triangles" can indicate potential market shifts. For example, an ascending triangle may suggest a bullish breakout, while a head-and-shoulders pattern often precedes a downward reversal.

Technical indicators enhance analysis by applying mathematical formulas to price, volume, or other data points. Moving averages, such as the 50-day and 200-day moving averages, help identify trends by smoothing out short-term fluctuations. A crossover between these averages might signal a buying or selling opportunity. Similarly, the Relative Strength Index (RSI) gauges whether an asset is overbought or oversold, while the Moving Average Convergence Divergence (MACD) highlights momentum changes.

Volume analysis is another key aspect of technical analysis. High trading volume accompanying price increases often signal strong investor interest, indicating a sustainable trend. Conversely, price movements on low volume suggest weaker market conviction. Monitoring volume alongside price can provide a clearer picture of market dynamics.

For long-term investors, technical analysis can identify favorable entry points, helping you maximize potential returns while minimizing risks. However, it's essential to remember that only some indicators are foolproof. Using multiple tools and integrating technical analysis with fundamental research ensures a more comprehensive evaluation of potential investments.

Combining Fundamental and Technical Insights

While each approach offers unique advantages, combining fundamental and technical analysis creates a more holistic view of a cryptocurrency's potential. Fundamental analysis identifies promising projects with strong long-term prospects, while technical analysis helps you time your investments effectively. For example, suppose your research indicates that a project addresses a significant market need and has robust community support. In that case, you might use technical indicators to determine the best moment to buy its token.

Consider a hypothetical scenario: You've identified a decentralized finance (DeFi) project with a compelling use case, an experienced team, and a growing community. The project's fundamentals suggest long-term viability, but the token's price has fluctuated. Technical analysis reveals that the asset is currently oversold according to its RSI, indicating a potential buying opportunity. By integrating both forms of analysis, you can make a well-informed decision that aligns with both short-term timing and long-term goals.

Tools to Support Your Analysis

A wealth of tools is available to help you conduct thorough research and analysis. Platforms like **CoinMarketCap** and **CoinGecko** offer real-time data on prices, market capitalization, and historical performance. These platforms are excellent starting points for evaluating coins and tracking trends.

Tools like **TradingView** provide advanced charting capabilities for deeper insights, allowing you to apply technical indicators and customize visualizations. Meanwhile, **Messari** delivers comprehensive research reports and financial metrics, making it a valuable resource for fundamental analysis.

On-chain analytics tools like **Glassnode** offer a unique perspective by analyzing blockchain data. Metrics such as active addresses, transaction volume, and wallet holdings provide clues about user adoption and network health. For example, a rise in active addresses on a blockchain may indicate growing interest and engagement, which could translate into increased demand for its token.

Using a combination of these tools empowers you to approach your investments with confidence. Each tool contributes to a broader understanding of market conditions, enabling you to effectively identify opportunities and manage risks.

Building Confidence Through Analysis
Investing in cryptocurrency requires more than intuition or reacting to market hype. Effective analysis builds confidence in your decisions, ensuring they are grounded in data and a deep market understanding. By committing to thorough research, you'll be better equipped to navigate the volatility of the crypto space and make choices that align with your long-term objectives.

Whether you're evaluating a promising new project or deciding when to enter a position, fundamental and technical analysis principles remain constant. Focus on the strength of a project's team, its use case's relevance, and its community's enthusiasm. Combine these insights with technical data to refine your strategy, and use trusted tools to support your research.

In the ever-evolving world of cryptocurrency, knowledge is your most valuable asset. By dedicating time to analyzing coins and projects, you position yourself to seize opportunities and minimize risks, building a portfolio that reflects your confidence and vision for the future. The following section will delve into portfolio management techniques to help you maintain balance and resilience as you continue your crypto investment journey.

Developing a Personal Strategy: A Practical Guide to Long-Term Crypto Success

Embarking on a journey in cryptocurrency investing requires more than enthusiasm; it demands a well-crafted strategy. Developing a personal investment strategy lays the groundwork for navigating the often volatile and unpredictable crypto markets. This approach ensures that your financial goals remain central, your portfolio reflects your risk tolerance, and your strategy evolves with changing conditions. A successful long-term strategy means setting clear goals, understanding the balance between risk and reward, and committing to regular evaluations and adjustments.

Setting Goals and Time Horizons

The first step in building a meaningful strategy is identifying what you want to achieve through cryptocurrency investing. These goals should be specific, actionable, and aligned with your broader financial picture. It's essential to ask yourself: Why am I investing in cryptocurrency? For some, the answer might be wealth accumulation over decades. Others may be looking for shorter-term gains or portfolio diversification.

Focusing on established projects like Bitcoin or Ethereum can be a prudent choice for those aiming to build wealth. These assets have demonstrated resilience and are less prone to extreme volatility than smaller altcoins. If passive income is your goal, exploring staking or yield farming through decentralized finance (DeFi) platforms could be worthwhile. However, weighing the potential rewards against the risks inherent in newer, less-proven technologies is crucial.

When defining your objectives, it's equally important to remain realistic. The allure of massive crypto gains can sometimes lead to unrealistic expectations. While overnight success stories are prevalent, they represent the exception rather than the rule. Cryptocurrencies are highly speculative assets, and achieving significant returns often requires patience and a commitment to long-term growth. Aligning your expectations with the reality of the market can help you remain focused and resilient.

Establishing a time horizon adds structure to your goals. Short-term objectives, such as saving for a major purchase, demand a focus on liquidity and lower-risk assets. Medium-term goals offer a balance, allowing you to explore mid-cap altcoins while maintaining exposure to stable, large-cap cryptocurrencies. For long-term aspirations, you have the luxury of riding out market volatility, enabling you to invest in higher-risk projects with significant growth potential. By anchoring your strategy to a defined timeline, you provide clarity and discipline to your decision-making process.

Balancing Risk and Reward
A successful investment strategy balances the potential for rewards with the realities of risk. This delicate equilibrium hinges on an honest assessment of your risk tolerance, which reflects your financial situation, experience, and emotional resilience to market swings. Knowing your comfort level with risk can guide how you allocate your resources and choose your investments.

For conservative investors, large-cap cryptocurrencies like Bitcoin and Ethereum often serve as a stabilizing force in the portfolio. Though not immune to volatility, these assets are less susceptible to dramatic swings than emerging altcoins. With their value pegged to fiat currencies, stablecoins can offer a haven during turbulent times, providing liquidity and a buffer against market downturns.

Moderate investors might diversify further, incorporating mid-cap altcoins into their portfolios. These coins, though riskier, present opportunities for growth, especially if tied to projects with solid fundamentals. An aggressive investor, willing to embrace high-risk, high-reward scenarios, might allocate a portion of their portfolio to small-cap tokens or newly launched projects. However, even for risk-tolerant people, diversification is essential. Spreading investments across different asset types minimizes the impact of any single underperforming asset.

Risk management tools like stop-loss orders can safeguard against steep losses. These mechanisms automatically sell an asset if its price falls to a predetermined level, allowing you to mitigate risk without constant market monitoring. Similarly, setting investment limits—regarding total exposure and allocations to specific assets—helps maintain balance in your portfolio and prevents overcommitment to any single strategy or coin.

Revisiting and Adjusting Your Strategy

The cryptocurrency market is not static, and neither should your strategy be. A successful investment plan requires periodic review and adaptation to remain relevant to your goals, risk tolerance, and market conditions. This process is not about making impulsive changes but staying aligned with your objectives as circumstances evolve.

Regularly monitoring market trends and developments is crucial. Many factors, including regulatory shifts, technological advancements, and macroeconomic events, shape the crypto landscape. By staying informed, you position yourself to anticipate changes that could impact your investments. Reliable news outlets like CoinDesk and CoinTelegraph are invaluable resources, offering insights into industry trends and updates.

Evaluating your portfolio's performance consistently allows you to identify assets that may no longer align with your strategy. If a coin consistently underperforms or deviates from your expectations, it might be time to reassess its place in your portfolio. Rebalancing is another essential practice—realigning your holdings to maintain your desired asset allocation ensures that your portfolio reflects your risk tolerance and investment objectives. For example, if a particular asset has appreciated significantly, it could dominate your portfolio, increasing your risk exposure. Rebalancing mitigates this by redistributing gains into other areas.

As your life circumstances change, so too should your strategy. Financial goals are not static, and shifts in income, family priorities, or career objectives can influence your approach to investing. Periodic reflection on your goals ensures that your strategy remains a true reflection of your aspirations. If your risk tolerance changes—perhaps due to market volatility or personal factors—adjustments to your portfolio can bring it back in line with your comfort level.

Flexibility is the hallmark of a resilient strategy. While remaining committed to your long-term goals is essential, being open to adjustments based on new information or market conditions is equally critical. For instance, shifting towards more stable assets in a prolonged bear market might protect your portfolio, while a bull market might present opportunities for higher-growth investments. Scaling in and out—gradually increasing or reducing your positions—can help you navigate market cycles without abrupt changes.

Crafting Your Personal Strategy
Developing a personal investment strategy is as much about introspection as it is about market analysis. Understanding what drives your decisions, what goals you hope to achieve, and how much risk you're willing to take creates a roadmap tailored

to your unique circumstances. Setting specific, measurable goals provides clarity and purpose while balancing risk and reward ensures that your portfolio reflects your aspirations and comfort level.

Revisiting and refining your strategy regularly keeps it relevant, adaptable, and aligned with your evolving financial landscape. The cryptocurrency market is unpredictable, but you can navigate its volatility with a structured, thoughtful approach with confidence and resilience. By staying focused on your goals, managing risk effectively, and embracing flexibility, you lay the foundation for long-term success in the ever-evolving world of crypto investing.

CHAPTER 9: STAYING UPDATED IN THE CRYPTO WORLD

The cryptocurrency landscape is dynamic, evolving at breakneck speed with new projects, technological advancements, and regulatory changes emerging daily. Staying informed is crucial for making educated investment decisions and responding effectively to market shifts. However, the sheer volume of information can be overwhelming, making it essential to develop strategies to filter noise, identify reliable updates, and maintain focus. You can confidently navigate this ever-changing ecosystem by leveraging trusted news sources, analyzing market trends critically, and staying emotionally balanced.

Following Market News and Trends

Keeping your finger on the pulse of the crypto market starts with identifying reliable sources of information. While numerous platforms claim to provide market insights, distinguishing trustworthy outlets from those spreading misinformation or hype is critical. Trusted news websites such as **CoinDesk** and **CoinTelegraph** are invaluable resources, offering timely articles on regulatory updates, blockchain innovations, and market trends. These platforms provide in-depth analyses and interviews with industry leaders, helping you understand the context behind price movements or project developments.

Social **media** platforms like Twitter can be a powerful tool for real-time updates. Key developers, analysts, and reputable influencers share insights faster than traditional outlets. However, verifying any claims before acting on them is vital, as social media can also be a breeding ground for misinformation. Reddit's active subreddits, such as r/cryptocurrency, provide a community-driven approach to news, where users discuss and debate emerging trends. While this can be useful for diverse perspectives, ensure you cross-reference information with established platforms.

For investors seeking a consolidated view, **news aggregators** like **CryptoPanic** offer a one-stop-shop for updates from multiple sources. Aggregators allow you to filter content based on sentiment—bullish, bearish, or neutral—making it easier to assess the market mood at a glance. Similarly, **CoinMarketCap and CoinGecko, while primarily price-tracking platforms,** offer curated news sections highlighting significant developments.

Podcasts and YouTube channels provide a more in-depth exploration of topics. Platforms like **The Pomp Podcast** and **Coin Bureau** delve into technical analyses, interviews, and educational content, offering perspectives on both macroeconomic trends and individual projects. Following a mix of these resources can build a comprehensive understanding of the crypto market.

Recognizing Hype vs. Real Developments

The crypto world thrives on excitement, but not all news is equal. Differentiating genuine developments from overblown hype is a skill that can save you from emotional, impulsive decisions. Start by examining the **source of** information. Reputable outlets with a track record of balanced reporting are more reliable than sensationalist blogs or anonymous social media posts.

When evaluating news, look for concrete details. For example, a partnership announcement backed by official statements from both parties carries more weight than vague promises of future collaboration. Similarly, technological upgrades like Ethereum's transition to Proof of Stake are significant because they address scalability and environmental concerns, improving the network's long-term viability. In contrast, announcements relying heavily on celebrity endorsements or vague promises of revolutionary potential often lack substance and serve primarily to generate short-term price spikes.

Analyzing the long-term impact of news is equally important. Developments that improve a project's adoption, security, or use case tend to have lasting value, whereas short-term marketing campaigns or speculative rumors often fade quickly. For instance, a project integrating its token into a widely used payment system has a measurable benefit, while vague claims of becoming "the next Bitcoin" are typically empty rhetoric.

Be cautious of projects focusing excessively on marketing while offering little technical or practical advancement. Examine their whitepaper, roadmap, and progress to ensure they align with their claims. When in doubt, prioritize projects with transparent teams and a history of delivering on promises.

Staying Calm Amidst Market Buzz

The emotional highs and lows of the crypto market can tempt even seasoned investors into reactive decision-making. Learning to maintain composure during periods of extreme volatility is essential for sticking to your long-term strategy.

Avoid emotional trading by setting clear rules for your investments. For instance, decide in advance the conditions under which you'll buy, sell, or hold an asset. Automated tools like stop-loss and take-profit orders can help enforce these rules, ensuring you act based on strategy rather than impulse. For example, a stop-loss order can protect you from significant losses during a sudden downturn, while a take-profit order locks in gains when an asset reaches a predetermined price.

It's also important to remind yourself of your long-term goals during moments of market turmoil. When prices are surging, it's easy to succumb to FOMO and buy at inflated levels, only to watch the market correct. Conversely, during downturns, panic can lead to selling assets at a loss. You can avoid these common pitfalls by focusing on your overall objectives.

Taking breaks from constant monitoring can also help you maintain perspective. The 24/7 nature of the crypto market can create pressure to stay perpetually informed, but this often leads to burnout. Limit your screen time and set specific periods for checking updates. In the meantime, shift your focus to research, learning, or other productive activities.

Finally, cultivate a **balanced perspective** by acknowledging that volatility is inherent in crypto investing. Short-term price swings don't define the long-term potential of a project. Celebrate wins without becoming overconfident, and treat losses as learning opportunities rather than failures.

Managing Information Overload
The sheer volume of information in the crypto world can be overwhelming. To stay focused, develop a structured approach to consuming news and insights. Start by curating a list of trusted sources, prioritizing those that align with your investment goals, and providing actionable information. Organize these resources into categories, such as general market updates, project-specific news, and technical analyses, to streamline your research process.

Consider subscribing to newsletters or setting up alerts for specific topics or assets. Many platforms, including CoinGecko and Messari, offer customizable notifications, ensuring you receive updates on areas that matter most to you. Avoid consuming every piece of news, as this can dilute your focus and lead to analysis paralysis.

Balancing depth with breadth is key. While staying updated on broad market trends is essential, diving deep into a smaller number of projects can provide a more meaningful understanding of their potential. If you've invested in specific assets, allocate time to studying their roadmaps, team updates, and community activity.

Building Confidence Through Knowledge
Knowledge is your greatest ally in navigating the crypto market. By continuously learning about blockchain technology, market mechanics, and emerging trends, you'll gain the confidence to make informed decisions. Dedicate time to expanding your understanding of fundamental concepts, such as decentralized finance (DeFi), non-fungible tokens (NFTs), and consensus mechanisms.

Participating in webinars, attending industry conferences, or joining online courses can deepen your expertise. Engaging with the crypto community through forums, social media, or local meetups offers opportunities to exchange ideas and learn from others' experiences.

Staying informed in the rapidly evolving world of cryptocurrency requires a blend of reliable information sources, critical thinking, and emotional discipline. Focus on trusted news platforms to ensure you get accurate and timely updates. Learn to separate genuine developments from overhyped claims and maintain a calm mindset during market fluctuations to avoid reactive decisions. Instead of consuming every piece of information, prioritize what aligns with your investment strategy. By adopting a structured approach to staying updated, you can confidently navigate the crypto market and make informed decisions in this dynamic and exciting space.

Understanding Technical Updates and Forks: Navigating Changes in the Crypto World
In the ever-evolving world of cryptocurrency, technical updates, and forks are pivotal events that can alter the course of blockchain networks. These changes may introduce new

features, enhance scalability, or resolve stakeholder ideological differences. Understanding these events is essential for investors, as they can influence market value, create new investment opportunities, or pose unforeseen risks. By diving into the nature of forks and their impact, you can equip yourself to navigate these complex phenomena with greater confidence.

Hard Forks vs. Soft Forks: The Nature of Blockchain Splits
At the heart of blockchain evolution lies the concept of forks, which occur when a blockchain's protocol undergoes changes. These changes, implemented by developers and validated by the community, can create two distinct outcomes: a permanent split or a backward-compatible upgrade. Understanding the difference between these types of forks is critical for anticipating their impact on the network and your investments.

A hard fork is a fundamental change to a blockchain protocol that is not backward-compatible. When a hard fork occurs, the network diverges into two chains, each with its distinct future. One of the most prominent examples of a hard fork is the creation of Bitcoin Cash (BCH) from Bitcoin (BTC). In this instance, disagreements over scalability—specifically, whether to increase block sizes to allow for faster transactions—led to a split. Bitcoin Cash emerged as a new blockchain, providing an alternative approach to scalability while retaining Bitcoin's shared history up to the point of divergence.

For investors, hard forks often bring opportunities in the form of new coins. Those holding the original cryptocurrency at the time of the fork typically receive an equivalent amount of the newly created coin, essentially doubling their holdings. However, the value of these new coins can vary widely, depending on market sentiment and the community's support for the forked project. Some coins, like Bitcoin Cash, have gained significant traction, while others have yet to find relevance.

On the other hand, soft forks are backward-compatible upgrades that allow all nodes, regardless of whether they adopt the changes, to remain part of the same blockchain. Soft forks often aim to introduce new features or address technical inefficiencies without causing a network split. A notable example is Bitcoin's Segregated Witness (SegWit) upgrade in 2017. SegWit enhanced transaction efficiency by altering how data is stored on the blockchain, reducing fees without creating a separate chain or coin.

Unlike hard forks, soft forks do not create new cryptocurrencies or cause community divisions. They tend to be less disruptive and more collaborative, allowing networks to evolve seamlessly. However, they still require consensus among miners, developers, and stakeholders to succeed. Understanding these distinctions between hard and soft forks helps you anticipate how they may influence your investments and the broader crypto ecosystem.

Why Forks Happen: The Driving Forces Behind Blockchain Changes
Forks are not random occurrences but deliberate actions taken to address challenges, implement upgrades, or resolve conflicts. By examining the motivations behind forks, you can better understand their potential impact on the network and your investment strategy.

Technical upgrades and improvements are among the most common reasons for forks. As blockchain networks grow and evolve, they often encounter scalability, transaction speed, or security limitations. Forks provide an opportunity to address these issues and introduce new features. For example, the Bitcoin Cash fork sought to enhance scalability by increasing block sizes, making transactions faster and more cost-effective for users. Similarly, security-focused forks may patch vulnerabilities or strengthen defenses against potential attacks, ensuring the network's long-term integrity.

Disagreements within a blockchain community can also lead to forks. These disputes may stem from differing opinions on governance, decentralization, or the project's philosophical direction. Ethereum's split into Ethereum (ETH) and Ethereum Classic (ETC) is a prime example. Following the infamous DAO hack, the Ethereum community debated whether to roll back the blockchain to reverse the hack's impact. While one faction prioritized immutability, the other supported intervention to protect investors. This disagreement resulted in two distinct blockchains, each embodying a different approach to governance and ethics.

Forks can also arise from the need to fix bugs or optimize network performance. In such cases, the changes are often technical and may take time to be noticeable to users. However, these adjustments are crucial for maintaining a blockchain's competitiveness and ensuring its functionality in a rapidly evolving market.

Finally, regulatory compliance can drive forks, mainly as governments introduce new cryptocurrency and blockchain technology rules. Privacy-focused coins like Monero, for instance, may undergo forks to align with regulations requiring transaction traceability. While rare, these compliance-driven forks highlight the growing intersection of blockchain technology and legal frameworks.

How Forks Impact Investors: Risks and Rewards
For investors, forks can be both exciting and uncertain. They often bring opportunities, such as creating new coins, but they can also introduce risks, including increased volatility and community divisions. By understanding these dynamics, you can make informed decisions about your portfolio during fork events.

One of the most direct benefits of a hard fork is the creation of new coins. When a blockchain splits, holders of the original cryptocurrency are typically rewarded with an equivalent amount of the new coin. This process resembles an airdrop and can offer potential gains if the new coin gains value. However, these opportunities come with caveats. Not all exchanges or wallets support the newly created coins, so it's essential to ensure that your holdings are in a compatible platform during the fork.

Forks often generate significant market volatility as traders and investors react to the potential implications of the split. Speculation in the lead-up to a fork can drive prices upward, while post-fork stabilization often reveals the true value of the affected coins. For example, Bitcoin's price experienced notable fluctuations during the Bitcoin Cash fork, reflecting optimism and uncertainty about the new chain's prospects.

Community divisions are another factor that can influence a project's future stability and, consequently, its investment appeal. A hard fork that exposes deep rifts within a community may erode confidence in the project's governance and long-term vision. Conversely, forks that resolve disputes or enhance functionality can strengthen a blockchain's position, attracting new users and investors.

It's also important to consider the tax implications of forks, which vary by jurisdiction. In some countries, receiving new coins due to a hard fork is treated as taxable income, with the fair market value determining the tax liability at the time of receipt. Consulting with a tax professional can help you navigate these complexities and avoid unexpected financial obligations.

Navigating Forks with Confidence
Staying informed is the key to navigating forks successfully. You can better assess its potential impact by following announcements from project teams, monitoring market sentiment, and understanding the technical and philosophical motivations behind a fork. Tools like CoinMarketCap,

CryptoPanic, and project-specific updates on GitHub or Medium can provide valuable insights into upcoming forks and their implications.

For long-term investors, forks represent an opportunity to evaluate the evolving dynamics of a blockchain project. By analyzing the community's response, the technical merits of the changes, and the market's reaction, you can make strategic decisions about whether to hold, sell, or diversify your portfolio. Remember that while forks can present exciting opportunities, they also require careful consideration to manage the associated risks effectively.

Understanding technical updates and forks is a crucial aspect of successful cryptocurrency investing. By grasping the differences between hard and soft forks, recognizing the motivations behind these events, and anticipating their impact on the market, you can confidently position yourself to navigate this dynamic landscape. As the crypto world evolves, staying proactive and informed will help you make the most of the opportunities that forks and technical updates present.

Leveraging Community Resources: Tapping into Collective Wisdom in Crypto

In the fast-paced cryptocurrency market, leveraging community resources is one of the most effective ways to stay informed and make well-rounded decisions. The crypto industry thrives on its decentralized, open-source ethos, with much of its innovation and knowledge being shared through public channels. From online forums to live events, the collective wisdom of the crypto community offers an unparalleled wealth of information. However, using these resources effectively requires discernment, engagement, and a strategic approach. You can unlock insights beyond price charts and headlines by actively participating in crypto communities, attending events, and following credible thought leaders.

Engaging with Crypto Communities: A Hands-On Approach
The heart of cryptocurrency lies in its communities, where developers, investors, and enthusiasts come together to share insights, debate ideas, and speculate on market trends. Platforms like Reddit and Twitter serve as dynamic hubs for these conversations, offering a blend of education, analysis, and camaraderie.

With its numerous crypto-focused subreddits, Reddit provides a space for in-depth discussions and a wide range of opinions. For beginners, subreddits like r/cryptocurrency offer general insights, while niche forums like r/bitcoin and r/ethereum delve into the specifics of individual projects. These spaces allow you to see how different community members view projects, their underlying technology, and market sentiment. However, it's essential to approach Reddit with a critical mindset.

While the platform's open nature fosters rich discussion, it also attracts misinformation and hype. When participating, don't hesitate to ask questions or seek clarification, as most communities welcome new voices and value genuine curiosity.

Twitter, on the other hand, delivers real-time updates and direct access to industry leaders. The platform's brevity fosters concise insights but also means you must sift through noise to find value. You can stay updated on the latest developments by following project accounts, developers, and influencers like Vitalik Buterin or Andreas Antonopoulos. Twitter Spaces further enriches this experience, enabling live, interactive discussions where you can listen to—and even engage with—key players in the industry. Engaging thoughtfully on Twitter, whether by sharing your insights or contributing to ongoing conversations, helps you build connections while staying informed.

Both platforms require a degree of media literacy. Verify any claims you encounter with reliable sources or official announcements, and avoid being swayed by sensationalist headlines or speculative posts. Communities can be powerful resources, but they are only as valuable as the effort you put into engaging critically and constructively.

Attending Events and Webinars: Learning from the Front Lines

While online communities provide a constant stream of information, events, and webinars, offer opportunities for deeper learning and personal interaction. These gatherings —whether virtual or in-person—bring together experts, developers, and investors to share insights, discuss trends, and explore the future of cryptocurrency.

Major conferences like Consensus by CoinDesk or ETHGlobal's hackathons attract top industry minds and provide a broad view of the blockchain landscape. These events often serve as launchpads for new technologies, partnerships, or regulatory discussions, making them essential for staying ahead of the curve. For instance, attending a decentralized finance (DeFi) session at Blockchain Expo might give you an edge in understanding how specific projects tackle scalability or regulatory challenges.

Webinars and online AMAs (Ask Me Anything sessions) have also become invaluable tools for engagement. Crypto projects often use these formats to share updates directly with their communities, allowing you to hear straight from the source. Platforms like Binance Academy or CoinGecko frequently host educational webinars on topics ranging from staking to smart contracts, helping you sharpen your technical understanding.

Preparation is vital to getting the most out of events and webinars. Familiarize yourself with the agenda, research speakers, and consider the questions you'd like to ask. Actively participating in Q&A sessions or engaging with other attendees can lead to new connections and insights. After the event, consolidate your notes and revisit recordings or presentation materials to reinforce your learning.

By attending events, you gain knowledge and access networking opportunities that can be critical for discovering new projects, collaborating with like-minded individuals, or even spotting trends before they become mainstream.

Following Reliable Thought Leaders: Finding Clarity in a Noisy World

In crypto, thought leaders play a pivotal role in shaping discourse and providing context to complex topics. These individuals often have deep expertise, whether as developers, analysts, or educators, and their insights can help you navigate the often-confusing world of blockchain and digital assets.

Notable figures like Vitalik Buterin, Charles Hoskinson, and Andreas Antonopoulos offer nuanced perspectives on blockchain innovation, governance, and adoption. Following them can deepen your understanding of cryptocurrency's technological and philosophical foundations. Similarly, financial analysts like Michael Saylor or Cathie Wood provide macroeconomic context, discussing how crypto fits into broader financial ecosystems.

When choosing thought leaders to follow, prioritize transparency and consistency. Reliable voices disclose their investments and provide balanced analyses highlighting opportunities and risks. Avoid influencers who focus on promoting specific coins without substantiating their claims, as they may be driven by personal gain rather than genuine insight.

Platforms like Twitter, LinkedIn, and YouTube are excellent channels for accessing thought leaders' content. For example, Guy from Coin Bureau provides detailed project reviews and market analyses on his YouTube channel, offering a balanced view that is particularly valuable for long-term investors. Podcasts like *The Pomp Podcast* by Anthony Pompliano or

Unchained by Laura Shin feature interviews with industry leaders, giving you a front-row seat to discussions on crypto's future.

Engage thoughtfully with these voices by asking questions, reflecting on their insights, and incorporating their perspectives into your research. Thought leaders can provide guidance, but your investment decisions should always align with your personal goals and understanding of the market.

Building a Balanced Approach to Community Engagement
The key to leveraging community resources effectively is balance. While online platforms, events, and thought leaders offer immense value, they can also overwhelm you with information or lead you into echo chambers. To avoid this, focus on quality over quantity. Curate your Reddit subscriptions and X following to include reliable sources that align with your interests. Schedule regular check-ins with these platforms rather than attempting to keep up with every update in real time.

Similarly, diversify your participation. Attend a mix of large-scale conferences for industry-wide insights and smaller webinars or meetups for more intimate discussions. When following thought leaders, seek various perspectives to avoid bias and develop a well-rounded understanding of the market.

By combining community engagement, event participation, and expert guidance, you can build a dynamic strategy for staying informed. This approach enhances your knowledge and connects you to the broader crypto ecosystem, empowering you to navigate its complexities with confidence.

Leveraging community resources is about more than gathering information—it's about participating actively in the crypto world. By engaging thoughtfully with platforms like Reddit and Twitter, attending events and webinars, and following credible thought leaders, you can stay ahead of market trends, deepen your understanding of blockchain technology, and build meaningful connections. These resources are tools and pathways to a more informed and empowered approach to cryptocurrency investing.

CHAPTER 10: THE FUTURE OF CRYPTOCURRENCY AND YOUR ROLE AS AN INVESTOR

The cryptocurrency space rapidly transforms global finance and asset ownership, with new technologies and applications emerging almost daily. As an investor, staying ahead of these trends is crucial for identifying opportunities and understanding the evolving market dynamics. The future of cryptocurrency is being shaped by three key trends: Decentralized Finance (DeFi), Non-Fungible Tokens (NFTs), the Metaverse, and Central Bank Digital Currencies (CBDCs). Each trend highlights different aspects of innovation within the financial ecosystem, presenting unique opportunities and challenges. Understanding these areas allows you to invest wisely and participate in shaping the future of finance.

Decentralized Finance (DeFi): Redefining Financial Systems
The rise of Decentralized Finance, or DeFi, has disrupted traditional financial systems by enabling peer-to-peer transactions without intermediaries like banks. At its core, DeFi uses blockchain technology and smart contracts to create financial products and services accessible to anyone with an internet connection. DeFi platforms offer a transparent, permissionless, and efficient alternative to traditional banking from lending and borrowing to earning interest through staking.

Imagine lending your assets through platforms like Aave or Compound and earning returns that outpace most savings accounts. Or consider borrowing against your cryptocurrency holdings without needing credit checks or lengthy approval processes. DeFi makes these scenarios a reality. Removing intermediaries reduces costs and creates opportunities for those who are excluded from traditional financial systems. In regions with limited banking infrastructure, DeFi can be a game-changer, offering financial access to millions who were previously underserved.

However, the DeFi space has its risks. The technology is relatively new and highly experimental, which leaves platforms vulnerable to hacks, coding errors, and exploitation. Smart contract vulnerabilities have already led to significant financial losses for some users. DeFi operates in a regulatory gray area, and increased government scrutiny could reshape how these platforms function. As an investor, you must tread carefully and perform due diligence on any platform before committing your assets.

Investing in DeFi can also be a way to earn passive income through yield farming or liquidity provision. These strategies involve providing assets to decentralized exchanges or protocols in exchange for rewards. While the returns can be attractive, they often come with risks, such as impermanent loss or market volatility. Diversifying your investments across multiple platforms and understanding the mechanics of each protocol are essential steps in managing these risks.

The future of DeFi holds immense potential, particularly as traditional financial institutions begin exploring ways to integrate DeFi concepts. By staying informed and engaging with this evolving ecosystem, you position yourself to capitalize on the opportunities DeFi offers while contributing to a more inclusive financial future.

NFTs and the Metaverse: Redefining Ownership and Interaction
The emergence of Non-Fungible Tokens (NFTs) and the

Metaverse has introduced groundbreaking changes in how we think about ownership and digital interaction. NFTs can tokenize unique assets, from digital art and music to virtual real estate and in-game items. This innovation has unlocked new revenue streams for creators and new investment opportunities for collectors and speculators.

NFTs derive their value from their uniqueness and verifiability on blockchain networks. Unlike cryptocurrencies such as Bitcoin, each NFT represents a specific item or asset, making it non-interchangeable. For artists, musicians, and brands, this technology allows them to reach audiences directly and monetize their creations without traditional intermediaries. For example, digital artist Beeple sold an NFT for over $69 million, demonstrating the market's potential to reshape the art world.

Beyond collectibles, NFTs are playing a crucial role in the Metaverse, a digital universe where people can interact in immersive virtual spaces. The Metaverse combines blockchain, virtual reality, and augmented reality technologies to create environments where NFTs represent everything from virtual land to digital clothing. Platforms like Decentraland and The Sandbox allow users to buy, sell, and develop virtual real estate, often turning these assets into monetizable experiences.

NFTs and the Metaverse offer immense potential for investors, but the market is also highly speculative. Prices are often driven by hype, and the long-term value of many NFTs remains uncertain. Researching the communities and ecosystems surrounding specific NFTs and projects is essential. For example, an NFT tied to a well-supported gaming platform may hold more lasting value than a standalone collectible.

The Metaverse, meanwhile, represents a longer-term investment opportunity. As major companies like Meta (formerly Facebook) invest billions into building virtual worlds, the demand for digital assets within these spaces will likely grow. Whether through virtual real estate, avatars, or Metaverse-native currencies, this emerging digital landscape offers a range of avenues for exploration.

To navigate this space effectively, focus on understanding the underlying technology and the potential use cases of the NFTs or Metaverse projects you're considering. Engage with the communities driving these innovations and look for projects demonstrating clear utility and sustainable growth models.

Central Bank Digital Currencies (CBDCs): Bridging the Gap Between Fiat and Digital Assets
While DeFi and NFTs emphasize decentralization, Central Bank Digital Currencies (CBDCs) represent a centralized approach to digital currency. CBDCs are digital versions of fiat currencies issued and regulated by central banks. Unlike cryptocurrencies, which are decentralized and often volatile, CBDCs offer the stability of traditional currencies combined with the efficiency of digital transactions.

Countries around the world are exploring or implementing CBDCs for various reasons. China's digital yuan is already in advanced testing, while the European Central Bank is actively researching the digital euro. The U.S. Federal Reserve has also begun examining the potential for a digital dollar. For governments, CBDCs offer several advantages, including faster cross-border transactions, reduced reliance on cash, and improved financial transparency.

CBDCs could transform the global financial system but raise significant questions about privacy and control. By design, CBDCs allow central banks to track and monitor transactions, which could enhance regulatory oversight and lead to government surveillance concerns. For consumers, the transition to CBDCs may change how money is stored and accessed, potentially reducing the role of commercial banks in the process.

From an investor's perspective, CBDCs present both challenges and opportunities. While they are unlikely to replace decentralized cryptocurrencies, CBDCs could coexist, each serving distinct purposes. For example, CBDCs might become the default for everyday transactions, while cryptocurrencies retain their appeal as investment vehicles or tools for decentralized finance.

CBDCs could also influence the broader cryptocurrency market. For instance, if CBDCs become integrated into DeFi platforms, they might create hybrid financial systems that combine the stability of government-backed currency with the innovation of decentralized protocols. Staying informed about CBDC developments will help you anticipate how these digital currencies impact your portfolio and the market as a whole.

Your Role as an Investor in the Evolving Landscape
The rise of DeFi, NFTs, the Metaverse, and CBDCs signals a shift in how we think about money, ownership, and financial interaction. As these trends unfold, your role as an investor is to navigate the opportunities and risks with a mindset of continuous learning and adaptability.

Start by educating yourself about each trend's underlying technology and market dynamics. Participate in discussions, attend events, and engage with the communities driving innovation. Staying informed will not only enhance your investment decisions but also allow you to contribute to the growth and direction of the industry.

Diversification is another critical element of your strategy. While it's tempting to focus on one area, such as DeFi or NFTs, spreading your investments across multiple sectors can help mitigate risk and capture opportunities across different trends. For example, allocate a portion of your portfolio to stable DeFi protocols, experiment with a few NFTs, and monitor CBDC developments for longer-term positioning.

Finally, approach this rapidly evolving market with a long-term perspective. Cryptocurrency is still in its early stages, and technologies that seem speculative today could become foundational. Balancing optimism with caution will help you navigate volatility while staying open to the possibilities of what's to come.

The future of cryptocurrency offers immense potential but demands diligence, curiosity, and a willingness to adapt. By understanding emerging trends like DeFi, NFTs, the Metaverse, and CBDCs, you position yourself as an investor and an active participant in shaping the next generation of finance and digital interaction. Your choices today will help define the role of these technologies in tomorrow's global economy. Stay informed, stay engaged, and embrace the journey ahead.

Preparing for Future Market Changes
The cryptocurrency market constantly evolves, presenting incredible opportunities and significant risks. With rapid innovation and increasing mainstream interest, the market of tomorrow may look vastly different from today. To navigate these changes successfully, it's essential to understand the key forces driving market transformation: market maturity and institutional adoption, technological advancements, and the balance of long-term opportunities and risks. By anticipating these developments and adapting your strategy, you can position yourself for success in this dynamic space.

Market Maturity and Institutional Adoption
Cryptocurrency, despite its growth, is still a relatively young market. Over the past decade, we've seen it transition from a niche concept embraced by early adopters to a global phenomenon with increasing interest from institutional players. This growing institutional involvement will significantly shape its future as the market matures.

In the early days of cryptocurrency, the market was dominated by retail investors and speculative traders, drawn by the promise of high returns and the allure of decentralization. Institutions were hesitant, citing concerns about volatility, regulatory ambiguity, and lack of infrastructure. However, the narrative shifted as the value proposition of digital assets became clearer. Companies like Tesla and Square made headlines with their Bitcoin investments, and financial giants like JPMorgan and Fidelity started offering cryptocurrency-related products.

Institutional adoption brings several benefits to the market. It provides much-needed legitimacy, attracting a broader audience of investors. With institutions comes greater liquidity, which can reduce the dramatic price swings that characterize crypto markets. Additionally, institutional interest drives robust infrastructure development, including secure custody solutions, advanced trading platforms, and compliance tools.

However, institutional adoption has its challenges. One concern is that the increased presence of large players may alter the market dynamics. Early crypto investors thrived in an environment of high volatility and speculative opportunities. As institutions stabilize prices and influence the market, some high-risk, high-reward opportunities may diminish. Furthermore, institutional involvement often brings heightened regulatory scrutiny as governments seek to integrate digital assets into traditional financial frameworks. While clear regulations can foster growth by building investor confidence, overly restrictive policies might stifle innovation and limit access for smaller players.

You can prepare for these changes by diversifying your portfolio as an investor. Established cryptocurrencies like Bitcoin and Ethereum will likely remain institutional favorites, offering stability and long-term growth potential. At the same time, consider allocating a portion of your investments to emerging projects that could deliver higher returns in this evolving market. Staying informed about regulatory developments and institutional trends will also help you make strategic decisions in this changing landscape.

Technological Innovations on the Horizon
Innovation is the lifeblood of the cryptocurrency market. The blockchain ecosystem is continuously evolving, with advancements that promise to reshape industries and expand the possibilities of digital assets. As an investor, understanding these technological developments is critical for identifying opportunities early and managing associated risks.

One of the most significant advancements in the pipeline is Ethereum 2.0. Ethereum has established itself as the leading platform for smart contracts and decentralized applications, but its scalability issues have limited its potential. Ethereum 2.0 addresses these challenges by transitioning to a proof-of-stake (PoS) consensus mechanism, reducing energy consumption, and introducing sharding to process transactions more efficiently. These improvements could make Ethereum more attractive to users and developers, potentially driving up the value of Ether (ETH).

Layer 2 solutions are another exciting development. These technologies are designed to work alongside existing blockchains to improve their scalability and reduce transaction costs. For example, the Lightning Network on Bitcoin and projects like Optimism and Arbitrum on Ethereum enable faster, cheaper transactions by processing them off-chain while maintaining the security of the main blockchain. As these solutions gain adoption, they could enhance the functionality of blockchain networks and attract new users.

Interoperability is another area of focus. Projects like Polkadot and Cosmos are working to create a seamless ecosystem where different blockchains can communicate and share data.

This "Internet of Blockchains" approach has the potential to break down silos within the crypto space, making digital assets more accessible and functional. For investors, supporting interoperability projects could offer exposure to a future where blockchain networks work together rather than compete.

Additionally, decentralized autonomous organizations (DAOs) are gaining traction as a new model for governance and decision-making. DAOs allow stakeholders to collectively manage projects, giving investors a voice in the direction of the projects they support. This model aligns incentives, fostering innovation and resilience within the ecosystem.

While these innovations bring exciting opportunities, they also come with risks. New technologies often face security challenges, including hacks and bugs. Moreover, the rapid pace of development means that projects must continuously adapt to stay relevant. As an investor, conduct thorough research into the teams and roadmaps behind these technologies. Diversify your investments across established projects and emerging innovations to balance the potential for high returns with the risk of obsolescence.

Long-Term Opportunities and Risks
The cryptocurrency market's long-term potential is vast, but it is accompanied by challenges that demand careful consideration. For investors, the key is to recognize both the opportunities for growth and the risks that could undermine them.

One of the most compelling opportunities is the potential for cryptocurrency to become a mainstream asset class. Today, digital assets are still considered alternative investments, but as institutional interest grows and infrastructure improves, they may become as commonplace as stocks or bonds. Projects addressing real-world challenges, such as enabling cross-border payments, enhancing data security, or democratizing finance, will likely thrive in this mature market.

Another opportunity lies in the global push for financial inclusion. Cryptocurrencies and blockchain technology can provide financial services to unbanked and underbanked populations, particularly in developing regions. Projects focused on microtransactions, low-cost remittances, and decentralized financial services have the potential to drive adoption while creating meaningful social impact.

However, the market also faces significant risks. Regulatory uncertainty remains a major concern. While many governments are moving toward more precise guidelines, the pace and nature of regulatory developments vary widely. Restrictive policies in key markets could limit innovation or exclude certain projects from participating in the global financial system. Staying informed about regulatory trends and diversifying across jurisdictions can help mitigate this risk.

Volatility is another challenge. Cryptocurrency prices are often influenced by speculation and market sentiment, leading to dramatic fluctuations. While this volatility can create opportunities for traders, it poses risks for long-term investors. Building a diversified portfolio and maintaining a long-term perspective can help weather these price swings.

Technological obsolescence is an additional concern. The rapid pace of innovation means that newer, more advanced technologies could overtake today's leading projects. As an investor, focus on projects with strong development teams, clear roadmaps, and the ability to adapt to changing market conditions. Keeping an eye on emerging trends and being willing to adjust your portfolio as needed will help you stay ahead.

Security also remains a critical issue. Despite advancements in blockchain technology, the market is still vulnerable to hacks, scams, and fraud. Secure wallets, choosing reputable exchanges, and conducting thorough due diligence on projects are essential for protecting your investments.

Navigating the Future
Preparing for future market changes requires a combination of vigilance, adaptability, and a commitment to continuous learning. The cryptocurrency market is dynamic, and staying ahead means keeping up with technological advancements, regulatory developments, and market trends. Diversify your portfolio to balance stability with growth potential and maintain a long-term perspective to navigate volatility.

Your ability to anticipate and adapt to changes will be critical as the market matures. By understanding the forces driving the evolution of cryptocurrency—whether through institutional adoption, groundbreaking technology, or new regulatory frameworks—you can position yourself to take advantage of the opportunities while managing the risks. In this way, you'll participate in the future of finance and help shape it.

Looking Ahead as a Prepared Investor
In the rapidly evolving world of cryptocurrency, your role as an investor extends far beyond merely holding assets and waiting for gains. Success in this space demands an active, informed, and adaptable approach that evolves in tandem with the market. Embracing institutional adoption, monitoring technological advancements, and maintaining a clear-eyed view of long-term risks and opportunities will set the foundation for sustained growth. More importantly, investing in your knowledge and strategy is as vital as investing in your portfolio. This chapter explores how you can reassess and refine your approach, build a mindset of continuous learning, and adapt to the ever-changing landscape of digital finance.

Reassessing and Refining Your Strategy
Cryptocurrency investing is anything but static. Markets change, technologies improve, and individual goals shift over

time. Regularly reassessing and refining your strategy ensures that your investments align with these dynamics while staying true to your objectives.

Take, for example, the experience of Chris, an early investor who initially focused on a simple buy-and-hold approach with Bitcoin and Ethereum. This strategy worked well for years as these assets dominated the market and steadily increased in value. However, as the crypto ecosystem expanded, Chris realized his portfolio needed more diversity and exposure to emerging sectors like DeFi and NFTs. A reassessment of his strategy revealed the need for a broader approach. Chris adjusted his portfolio to allocate portions to new technologies and projects while keeping the majority in reliable, established cryptocurrencies.

Regular reflection on your portfolio and strategy is essential. Periodic reviews—quarterly or biannually—allow you to assess how well your investments perform and whether they reflect current trends and market conditions. Ask yourself critical questions: Are your holdings diversified enough to mitigate risk? Are they aligned with your risk tolerance? Do they take advantage of emerging opportunities? The answers can guide adjustments that keep your strategy relevant.

Diversification plays a crucial role in maintaining a resilient portfolio. While Bitcoin and Ethereum may remain foundational assets, expanding into areas like stablecoins, governance tokens, or even staking opportunities can provide stability and growth potential. Proper diversification goes beyond asset variety; it also means balancing short-term opportunities, such as yield farming, with long-term investments in transformative technologies.

Practical tools, such as setting target prices or implementing stop-loss orders, can also help safeguard your investments. Stop-loss orders, for instance, automatically sell assets if their value drops to a certain level, protecting you from severe losses during market downturns. Similarly, taking profits at predetermined levels ensures that gains are realized rather than lost to sudden volatility. By refining your strategy, you maintain flexibility, enabling you to adapt to the market's fluctuations and capitalize on its growth.

Building Knowledge for Continuous Growth
In cryptocurrency, staying informed is not just helpful—it's essential. The rapid pace of innovation and market change means that ongoing education is one of your most valuable assets. Committing to continuous learning will empower you to make better decisions, identify emerging trends, and confidently navigate the complexities of digital finance.

Sarah's journey illustrates the power of this approach. Starting as a novice investor, she dedicated herself to understanding blockchain technology and the intricacies of the market. Each week, she explored a specific topic—beginning with Bitcoin's fundamentals before moving on to DeFi protocols, staking, and NFTs. She consumed content from reputable sources like CoinDesk, followed thought leaders on Twitter, and joined Telegram groups to engage with the crypto community. This steady accumulation of knowledge transformed her from a hesitant beginner to a confident investor with a well-rounded perspective.

To replicate this growth, focus on diverse learning resources. Podcasts like *Unchained* or *The Pomp Podcast* offer expert commentary on current trends, while newsletters from platforms like Binance Academy provide bite-sized insights into complex topics. Whitepapers and project websites, though more technical, are invaluable for understanding the vision and mechanics behind specific cryptocurrencies or protocols.

Exploring beyond your immediate interests can also be rewarding. Even if you primarily invest in established cryptocurrencies, learning about areas like decentralized autonomous organizations (DAOs) or interoperability projects can open your eyes to how these technologies interact with the broader ecosystem. The more you understand, the better equipped you'll be to spot opportunities and assess risks.

Making learning a habit ensures that you remain agile in a fast-changing market. Dedicating small, consistent blocks of time—whether daily or weekly—can make the process less overwhelming. Focus on depth rather than breadth, diving deeply into one topic at a time to build a strong foundation. Continuous growth isn't about mastering everything overnight; it's about steadily equipping yourself with the knowledge to succeed.

Embracing the Evolution of Crypto Markets
The cryptocurrency market is inherently dynamic. From regulatory changes to technological breakthroughs, it is constantly reshaping itself. Embracing this evolution with an open mind and a willingness to adapt is critical for long-term success.

Michael's experience underscores this principle. A long-time Bitcoin investor, Michael initially hesitated to engage with newer trends like DeFi or NFTs. However, as these areas became prominent, he realized that ignoring them limited his perspective—and his portfolio's potential. Instead of dismissing these innovations as speculative fads, Michael took the time to understand their use cases and potential impact. He diversified his investments to include promising projects in these spaces, positioning himself to benefit from the market's expansion.

Change is inevitable in cryptocurrency, whether it's the rise of Central Bank Digital Currencies (CBDCs), blockchain scalability advancements, or regulatory frameworks shifts. Each development presents an opportunity to refine your approach. For example, CBDCs could influence the demand for decentralized cryptocurrencies, while Layer 2 solutions like the Lightning Network may enhance the utility of existing blockchains. Understanding these trends enables you to anticipate their impact and adjust accordingly.

Regulatory developments, in particular, demand close attention. Governments worldwide are working to integrate cryptocurrencies into their financial systems, introducing laws that could reshape the market. While regulations might initially seem restrictive, they often bring stability and clarity, encouraging broader adoption. Staying informed about these changes helps you align your investments with compliant and forward-thinking projects, avoiding potential pitfalls.

Finally, volatility is a defining feature of crypto markets. Price swings can be unsettling but are also a hallmark of an emerging asset class. By adopting a long-term perspective, you can view volatility as an opportunity rather than a threat. Use market dips to buy assets at lower prices and avoid making emotional decisions during sudden spikes or crashes. Maintaining composure and focusing on the bigger picture will help you confidently navigate these fluctuations.

Your Role in the Future of Cryptocurrency
As the crypto market grows, so does your responsibility as an investor. This journey isn't just about tracking prices or following trends—it's about actively participating in a transformative movement. Whether investing in decentralized finance, exploring the Metaverse, or watching the rollout of CBDCs, your decisions contribute to shaping the future of finance.

To succeed, cultivate curiosity, adaptability, and discipline. Stay informed by engaging with communities, following thought leaders, and continuously building your knowledge. Reassess your strategy regularly, ensuring it evolves with the market and your personal goals. Diversify thoughtfully, balance stability with growth, and always approach new opportunities optimistically and cautiously.

The future of cryptocurrency is bright, but it's also uncertain. By preparing for change and embracing the dynamic nature of the market, you can position yourself to thrive in this exciting era of digital finance. Your role as an investor isn't just to react to the market—it's to navigate its evolution with confidence, foresight, and purpose.

Crypto Investor's Checklist: Navigating the Market
The cryptocurrency world is dynamic, fast-paced, and full of opportunities—but it also demands careful planning, consistent learning, and disciplined execution. This checklist distills the core strategies and principles outlined in the book into actionable steps, offering a practical framework to guide your journey as a crypto investor. Whether you're a beginner building a foundation or an experienced trader refining your approach, this checklist will help you stay organized, focused, and prepared to adapt to the evolving market. Use it as a reference to align your decisions with your goals, safeguard your assets, and thrive in the future of digital finance.

The Comprehensive Cryptocurrency Success Checklist provides an actionable roadmap for navigating the dynamic world of digital assets. Begin by defining your purpose, whether it's long-term growth, passive income, or portfolio diversification, while assessing your risk tolerance to align investments with your comfort level. Secure your trading experience by selecting a reputable exchange and activating robust security measures, including two-factor authentication and strong passwords. To maximize returns, focus on diversifying your portfolio with a mix of established cryptocurrencies and emerging projects.

Effective portfolio management is key to success. Regularly monitor your investments using tools like CoinGecko or Blockfolio, and employ dollar-cost averaging to counteract market volatility. Implement stop-loss and take-profit orders to automate risk management and secure gains, and maintain balance by rebalancing your portfolio quarterly to stay aligned with your strategy.

Staying informed is essential in the fast-moving crypto world. Rely on trusted sources such as CoinDesk and CoinTelegraph for updates, and engage with online communities on platforms like Reddit, Telegram, and Twitter for diverse perspectives. Participate in events and webinars like Consensus and ETHGlobal to expand your knowledge and network. Finally, remain vigilant about regulatory updates, ensuring compliance and staying ahead of changes that could impact your investments. This structured approach empowers you to navigate the cryptocurrency landscape confidently and effectively.

Conclusion

The future of cryptocurrency represents a profound shift in how we perceive finance, ownership, and digital interaction. As blockchain technology evolves, it is poised to redefine industries, empower individuals, and create a more inclusive financial ecosystem. This transformation offers investors immense opportunities but demands a strategic and adaptive approach. By understanding key trends such as Decentralized Finance (DeFi), Non-Fungible Tokens (NFTs), the Metaverse, and Central Bank Digital Currencies (CBDCs), you can position yourself not just to benefit financially but also to contribute to the broader adoption and evolution of these technologies.

DeFi unlocks financial systems once restricted by geographical and institutional barriers, enabling greater access and efficiency. Meanwhile, NFTs and the Metaverse are redefining ownership, creativity, and interaction in digital spaces, signaling a shift toward more immersive and decentralized digital economies. CBDCs, on the other hand, bridge the gap between traditional finance and digital innovation, offering stability while fostering regulatory integration. These trends reflect the growing convergence of technology and finance, presenting opportunities that were unthinkable just a decade ago.

However, with these opportunities come challenges. Cryptocurrency markets remain volatile, speculative, and heavily influenced by technological and regulatory developments. As an investor, navigating these complexities requires diligence, continuous learning, and a long-term perspective. Embrace the dynamism of the market by staying informed through credible sources, engaging with communities, and leveraging analytical tools to guide your decisions. Diversifying your portfolio across different sectors and maintaining a balance between established assets and emerging technologies will help mitigate risks and capture growth.

Moreover, adaptability is key. The crypto space is still in its infancy, with innovations constantly reshaping the landscape. Projects that are speculative today could become foundational tomorrow. Regularly reassessing your strategy, staying ahead of technological advancements, and being attuned to regulatory changes are critical for staying relevant in this fast-paced environment.

Your role as an investor extends beyond profit-making; it involves participating in a transformative movement shaping the future of global finance. Every decision you make—supporting DeFi protocols, acquiring NFTs, or monitoring the integration of CBDCs—contributes to the evolution of a decentralized and digital-first economy. This participation underscores the importance of curiosity, discipline, and resilience.

The cryptocurrency market is as much about vision and innovation as capital. By approaching it with foresight and responsibility, you can navigate its volatility while embracing its boundless potential. As blockchain technology continues to disrupt and inspire, your ability to adapt, learn, and invest wisely will determine your success in this transformative era. The future of cryptocurrency is bright, unpredictable, and full of possibilities—and as an informed and strategic investor, you have the opportunity to be at the forefront of shaping this exciting new frontier.

Stay caught up as the digital world accelerates. "The Crypto Compass" points to financial growth, technological discovery, and a deeper understanding of the forces shaping tomorrow. The future of finance isn't just coming—it's already here. It's time to chart your course.

References

Sources for insights and foundational knowledge in The Crypto Compass: Charting Your Path in a Digital World include seminal texts such as Mastering Bitcoin: Unlocking Digital Cryptocurrencies by Andreas M. Antonopoulos and authoritative articles from CoinDesk, CoinTelegraph, and academic research on blockchain technology and decentralized finance. For historical and technical details, references to Satoshi Nakamoto's original whitepaper, Bitcoin: A Peer-to-Peer Electronic Cash System, were foundational to understanding Bitcoin's creation and principles.

Chapter 1 and 2 provides insights and information from various respected resources, including Mastering Bitcoin: Unlocking Digital Cryptocurrencies by Andreas M. Antonopoulos, for foundational knowledge on Bitcoin and blockchain technology. Additional context on Ethereum and altcoins is informed by the Ethereum whitepaper, authored by Vitalik Buterin, and articles from CoinDesk, CoinTelegraph, and Binance Academy, which offer in-depth analyses of market trends, technological advancements, and emerging cryptocurrencies. Historical and technical details about key cryptocurrencies and blockchain technology innovations are grounded in the original Bitcoin whitepaper, Bitcoin: A Peer-to-Peer Electronic Cash System, by Satoshi Nakamoto.

The content and recommendations in chapter 3 draw on established resources like Binance Academy and CoinDesk for wallet security best practices, as well as the insights provided by hardware wallet manufacturers such as Ledger and Trezor, which outline secure wallet setup and use. The chapter also incorporates concepts from Andreas M. Antonopoulos's Mastering Bitcoin: Unlocking Digital Cryptocurrencies, which explains the importance of securing private keys and managing digital wallets. Additionally, real-world advice reflects guidance shared on platforms like CryptoCompare and Trust Wallet's Help Center, which offer user-friendly tutorials for beginners entering cryptocurrency.

The content in chapter 4 draws on resources from prominent platforms like Binance Academy and Coinbase Learn, which provide comprehensive guides on centralized and decentralized exchanges, account setup, and security best practices. Additional insights are derived from Andreas M. Antonopoulos's Mastering Bitcoin: Unlocking Digital Cryptocurrencies and Chris Burniske and Jack Tatar's Cryptoassets: The Innovative Investor's Guide to Bitcoin and Beyond. These references explain the operational models of exchanges, risk management, and the evolving role of cryptocurrency trading platforms in the digital economy. Practical advice for securing accounts reflects recommendations from organizations such as CryptoCompare and Kraken Support Center, emphasizing user education on two-factor authentication, phishing prevention, and custodial versus self-custodial solutions.

The insights in chapter 5 draw on resources such as Binance Academy and Coinbase Learn, which provide detailed guides on trading strategies, market orders, and budget planning for cryptocurrency beginners. Additional inspiration is taken from Andreas M. Antonopoulos's Mastering Bitcoin: Unlocking Digital Cryptocurrencies for foundational blockchain knowledge and Chris Burniske and Jack Tatar's Cryptoassets: The Innovative Investor's Guide to Bitcoin and Beyond, which explores portfolio management and investment psychology. Tools like CoinMarketCap, CoinGecko, and educational platforms like Investopedia also contribute practical advice for tracking investments and understanding market dynamics.

Chapter 6 draws insights from multiple expert resources, including "Cryptoassets: The Innovative Investor's Guide to Bitcoin and Beyond" by Chris Burniske and Jack Tatar, which offers practical risk management strategies for cryptocurrency investments. The importance of diversification and dollar-cost averaging is highlighted in resources such as Coinbase Learn and Binance Academy, which provide foundational and advanced cryptocurrency education. Additional analysis of market volatility and emotional investing is informed by Andreas M. Antonopoulos's Mastering Bitcoin, and historical context on market crashes stems from articles and data featured on CoinDesk and CryptoSlate. Security practices were cross-referenced with recommendations from Ledger's blog and Trezor's security guides.

Chapter 7 draws insights from official tax documentation, such as the Internal Revenue Service (IRS) guidance on virtual currency transactions, particularly the FAQ on crypto taxation (IRS Notice 2014-21 and subsequent updates). Tools like CoinTracker and Koinly were referenced for their best practices in crypto tax software and record-keeping solutions. Key information on international regulations and trends was informed by resources from CoinDesk, CryptoSlate, and the European Commission's Markets in Crypto-Assets (MiCA) regulation proposal. Context on global regulatory frameworks was supplemented by insights from the OECD's reports on digital assets taxation and articles in Bloomberg Crypto.

Chapter 8 incorporates insights from resources like "The Bitcoin Standard" by Saifedean Ammous, which explores the long-term value of cryptocurrencies, and "Cryptoassets: The Innovative Investor's Guide to Bitcoin and Beyond" by Chris Burniske and Jack Tatar, which outlines strategies for building a diversified and resilient crypto portfolio. Industry tools and analytics platforms such as CoinMarketCap, CoinGecko, and TradingView provided guidance on technical and fundamental analysis. Thought leadership articles from CoinDesk, The Block, and CryptoSlate were used to contextualize trends and strategies in the ever-evolving crypto market. On-chain analytics insights were supported by data from platforms like Glassnode and Messari.

Chapter 9 draws insights from a combination of authoritative resources, including "The Bitcoin Standard" by Saifedean Ammous, which discusses the evolving role of cryptocurrency; trusted industry news platforms such as CoinDesk, CoinTelegraph, and Decrypt, which provide up-to-date coverage of market trends, regulatory changes, and technological advancements; and educational podcasts like "Unchained" by Laura Shin and "The Pomp Podcast" by Anthony Pompliano, which offer expert interviews and macroeconomic context. Analysis of community platforms like Reddit and Twitter, as well as tools such as CryptoPanic for aggregated news and sentiment analysis, informed strategies for effective engagement with market developments. Finally, foundational knowledge of blockchain mechanics and updates stems from resources on platforms like Ethereum.org and Messari.

Chapter 10 synthesizes insights from industry-leading resources, including "The Infinite Machine" by Camila Russo, which details the transformative potential of Ethereum and decentralized finance; reputable platforms like CoinDesk, CoinTelegraph, and Decrypt for up-to-date analysis on NFTs, the Metaverse, and Central Bank Digital Currencies (CBDCs); and academic perspectives on blockchain adoption, such as those found in research by The MIT Digital Currency Initiative. Podcasts like "Unchained" by Laura Shin and industry reports from Messari and Chainalysis contributed to discussions on institutional adoption and long-term trends. Tools like Glassnode and CoinMarketCap provided quantitative insights into DeFi and emerging blockchain solutions. Additionally, global economic reports on CBDC trials, including those from the Bank for International Settlements (BIS), informed the analysis of regulatory and financial integration.

Index

A
Active Investing

Characteristics and demands, 60–61
Balancing with passive strategies, 63
Advantages and risks, 61
Airdrops

Definition, 83
Tax implications, 83
Algorithmic Stablecoins

Overview and purpose, 28
Risks and vulnerabilities, 28–29
Altcoins

Role in diversification, 49, 62
Risk-reward balance, 50
Examples of mid-cap and small-cap altcoins, 50
AML/KYC Requirements

Importance in crypto exchanges, 87
Impact on privacy, 88
Averaging Strategies

Dollar-cost averaging (DCA), 22, 61

B
Bear Markets

Historical examples, 34
Lessons learned, 34–35

Strategies for surviving downturns, 78
Bitcoin (BTC)

As a store of value, 48, 68
Institutional adoption, 96
Hard forks and Bitcoin Cash, 134
Blockchain

Technology overview, 22, 94
Applications in DeFi, 103
Role in NFTs, 108
Borrowing in DeFi

Platforms and mechanisms, 103
Bubble Cycles

Recognizing and managing risks, 28, 34

C

Candlestick Charts

Use in technical analysis, 69
Capital Gains

Tax implications and reporting, 82–83
Short-term vs. long-term gains, 82
Central Bank Digital Currencies (CBDCs)

Overview and global development, 113
Impact on crypto markets, 115
Regulatory considerations, 114
Community Engagement

Leveraging forums and discussions, 138–139
Benefits for research and collaboration, 75
Cryptocurrency Wallets

Types (hot vs. cold), 90
Security best practices, 90

D

Decentralized Autonomous Organizations (DAOs)

Definition and governance models, 93
Examples in DeFi, 93
Decentralized Exchanges (DEXs)

Advantages and challenges, 23, 106
Decentralized Finance (DeFi)

Overview and significance, 102–104
Lending and borrowing platforms, 103
Yield farming and liquidity provision, 103
Integration with CBDCs, 116
Diversification

Importance in portfolio management, 49, 64
Strategies for reducing risk, 49, 64

E
Ethereum (ETH)

Smart contracts and dApps, 22, 69
Ethereum 2.0 and scalability, 93
Emotional Investing

Managing FOMO and panic selling, 78
Tools to maintain discipline, 78
Emerging Trends

DeFi, NFTs, and Metaverse, 102, 110

F
Fiat On-Ramps

Bridging traditional and digital finance, 106
Forks

Hard forks vs. soft forks, 133–134
Case studies: Bitcoin Cash and Ethereum Classic, 134–135
Investor impact, 135
FOMO (Fear of Missing Out)

Recognizing triggers, 78

Strategies to avoid impulsive decisions, 78
Fundamental Analysis

Evaluating project viability, 68
Factors to assess (team, use case, community), 68

H

Hack Prevention

Lessons from major crypto hacks, 31
Security best practices, 90
Hard Forks

Definition and examples, 133–134
Impact on investors, 135
High-Risk Investments

Identifying and managing, 50

I

Initial Coin Offerings (ICOs)

Overview and risks, 28
Examples of successes and failures, 28
Institutional Adoption

Drivers and impact, 95–96
Regulatory influence, 96
Interoperability

Benefits for blockchain networks, 94
Leading projects (Polkadot, Cosmos), 94

L

Layer 2 Solutions

Improving scalability, 94
Examples: Lightning Network, Optimism, Arbitrum, 94
Learning Resources

Recommended platforms and podcasts, 140
Educational tools for beginners, 140
Liquidity Pools

Functionality in DeFi, 103
Risks (impermanent loss), 103
M
Market Cycles

Historical insights and trends, 34
Timing investment decisions, 34
Metaverse

Investment Opportunities, 109
Role of NFTs in virtual worlds, 109
Mining Rewards

Tax implications, 83
N
Non-Fungible Tokens (NFTs)

Applications in art and gaming, 108
Integration with Metaverse, 109
Risks and market volatility, 109
P
Passive Investing

Characteristics and benefits, 61–62
Combining with active strategies, 63
Portfolio Management

Balancing risk and reward, 50, 63
Strategies for reassessment, 142
Proof-of-Stake (PoS)

Benefits and examples, 93
R
Regulatory Landscape

Global trends and challenges, 87
Implications for DeFi and NFTs, 89
S
Scalability

Blockchain challenges and solutions, 94
Security

Best practices for investors, 90
Using hardware wallets, 90
Smart Contracts

Role in DeFi, 103
Risks of coding vulnerabilities, 103
Stablecoins

Use cases and risks, 49, 104
T
Tax Compliance

Reporting capital gains, 82–83
Tools for tax preparation, 85
Technical Analysis

Key tools and indicators, 69
Importance for timing investments, 69
V
Volatility

Managing through diversification, 77
Tools to mitigate risks, 96
Whale Activity

Market impact and implications, 25
Yield Farming

Strategies and risks, 103

www.ingramcontent.com/pod-product-compliance
Lightning Source LLC
Chambersburg PA
CBHW071540220526
45469CB00003B/864